God's Best Friend

MW01672716

God's Best Friend

A BIG GOD
A SMALL HUMAN
AND A NAUGHTY DOG

Clay Cornelius

TATE PUBLISHING
AND ENTERPRISES, LLC

God's Best Friend
Copyright © 2011 by Clay Cornelius. All rights reserved.

No part of this publication may be reproduced, stored in a retrieval system or transmitted in any way by any means, electronic, mechanical, photocopy, recording or otherwise without the prior permission of the author except as provided by USA copyright law.

Scripture quotations marked (KJV) are taken from the *Holy Bible, King James Version*, Cambridge, 1769. Used by permission. All rights reserved.

Scripture quotations marked (NASB) are taken from the *New American Standard Bible®*, Copyright © 1960, 1962, 1963, 1968, 1971, 1972, 1973, 1975, 1977, 1995 by The Lockman Foundation. Used by permission.

Scripture quotations marked (NIV) are taken from the *Holy Bible, New International Version®*, NIV®. Copyright © 1973, 1978, 1984 by Biblica, Inc.™ Used by permission of Zondervan. All rights reserved worldwide. www.zondervan.com

Scripture quotations marked (NLT) are taken from the *Holy Bible, New Living Translation*, copyright © 1996. Used by permission of Tyndale House Publishers, Inc., Wheaton, Illinois 60189. All rights reserved.

The opinions expressed by the author are not necessarily those of Tate Publishing, LLC.

Published by Tate Publishing & Enterprises, LLC
127 E. Trade Center Terrace | Mustang, Oklahoma 73064 USA
1.888.361.9473 | www.tatepublishing.com

Tate Publishing is committed to excellence in the publishing industry. The company reflects the philosophy established by the founders, based on Psalm 68:11,
"The Lord gave the word and great was the company of those who published it."

Book design copyright © 2011 by Tate Publishing, LLC. All rights reserved.
Cover design by Shawn Collins
Interior design by Nathan Harmony

Published in the United States of America

ISBN: 978-1-61346-921-7
Religion / Christian Life / General
11.11.29

Table of Contents

Foreword **9**

Introduction **11**

An Unlikely Teacher 13

The Blonde Bulldozer 19

Part 1: God's Existence and Attributes: The Laws of Nature

Jenna's Guillotine 27

Pound Puppies 33

Light Years Ahead 41

Power and Play 47

Jenna's Poop and God's Justice 51

Part 2: God and Mankind: The Laws of the Land

God the President 59

Moments of Truth 65

Swat Team 71

Stuck Together 77

Bed Bugged 83

Part 3: God and Community: The Purpose of the Church

God the Boss 91

Mr. and Mrs. Pack Man 99
A Tight Leash 105
Stinky Jenna 111
Deeper Waters 117

Part 4: God and the Individual: The Importance of the Bible

God the Friend 125
The Manual that Overrides 131
Hearing Repaired 137
The Lame Name 143
The Jenglish Language 149
God's Best Friend 155

Part 5: God and the Child: The Significance of Two-Way Communication (Prayer)

God the Father 163
The Length of Longing 171
Triple Treats 179
The God Box 189
Unleashed 197
Creature from Beyond 203

Part 6: God and the Complete Human, Birth through Death: The Salvation Plan

God the Savior 213
The Tumor 223
Choosing Sacrifice 231
God's Un-Understandable Plan 239
Anger and Anguish 249

Part 7: God and the Human Spirit: Eternal Laws and Purpose

God the Spirit. 259

Release 269

The Ritual Tricks 277

Full Circle 285

Conclusion 291

About the Author 295

Foreword

Author Clay Cornelius possesses a unique gift of presenting spiritual truths from everyday illustrations and experiences. He admits that he learned most of his lessons from "the streets." No wonder he connects with his readers.

Get ready for an adventure with Jenna, a yellow Labrador retriever, that will lead you on another kind of adventure—an experience in relationship with the Creator Himself. You'll be touched by Clay's journey in discovering that God exists. You'll laugh at some of the stories, like the nightmare incident with Herman the goldfish. In that too, Clay finds a principle—a deeper truth—to be presented to his readers. *God's Best Friend* explores the depths of our coexistence with God and how we play a role in making that coexistence a positive experience. Everyone seems to have a concept about what it means to "work for God." Clay explores the myths many espouse, answering questions quite typical to the believer—questions like:

- Why doesn't God answer all my prayers?
- How do we receive rewards from God?
- Can I trust God to give me something good?
- Where did God get all His knowledge—from the Internet?
- What are some of life's deceptions?

- Is it possible that somewhere along the line I allowed my conscience to be altered?
- Why am I squirming when I say I'm trusting the Lord?
- How do I smell to God? Do I exude a spiritually nasty smell?

God's Best Friend is a scholarly, fun, touching, and non-religious approach to developing a trusting relationship with God.

Thanks, Clay, for your influence.

—Dr. Dave Williams
Pastor and Author, Mount Hope Church, Lansing, MI

Introduction

"I believe in God," I told an atheist friend years ago as he passed me the joint. My announcement seemed to me like a bold statement, but it really wasn't. In America a person is simply agreeing with the majority when he says, "I believe in God." I got kind of a moderate warm fuzzy when I said it back then. I felt like I was doing my part to promote good, if nothing more than being a spiritual optimist. And then I got high, got drunk, and went looking for girls. I guess I hoped this "God" wasn't paying attention…

My revelry went great for a while. But you know, life has a tendency to get a little bit rough. Eventually, I needed more than just a vague statement and a warm fuzzy. I needed some serious help. My recreational habits turned into addictions, and addictions turned into depression. Depression got me thinking about death—escaping all life's struggles for good. And suddenly I hoped that God *was* paying attention.

My theology regarding death at that time went something like this: When we die, we're all herded into an oversized dog pound, each person with an individual cell. And maybe we sit there for a while, and then in comes God. As soon as we see him, everyone gets up and jumps and flails and shouts, "Pick me! Pick me!" God walks through the many kennels, with his hand on his chin, pondering deeply. And when he looks at me, maybe if my cage isn't too loaded with poop, and maybe if I give him just the right puppy-dog eyes, he will pick me to go to heaven. I hoped I would be so lucky.

So there it was; my great hope for the future was based on the off chance that God preferred using brown-haired, brown-eyed, five-foot-ten drug addicts to populate his kingdom. No wonder I was so depressed. I had nothing but self-formulated God theories and a persistent hopeless feeling. But I wanted the truth. I wanted to know what I could do to get to heaven when I died. More practically, I wanted to know what I could do to get out of the mess I had made of my life. Ultimately, I wanted to find God. I *needed* to find God.

Well, my search didn't disappoint—not at all. And the results of that search are contained in this book. If there is any way we can understand God or get on his good side, we need to know about it. It's the key to a better life. You may have picked up this book because you like philosophizing, or perhaps because you like silly pet stories, and either way you won't be disappointed. But if you realize that you need something more in life, something only God can provide, then this book is just for you. If you are truly seeking God, you will undoubtedly find him.

> Ask and it will be given to you; seek and you will find; knock and the door will be opened to you.
>
> Matthew 7:7 (NIV)

An Unlikely Teacher

As I began my search for the truth about God, the first thing I realized was that I felt grossly unqualified to conduct such an investigation. I thought to myself, *I'm just an average guy; how am I supposed to understand the "wisdom of the ages"?* If all the high-level theology professors in the world couldn't come to a consensus, how could some insignificant non-scholar like me ever reach a conclusion? I am an example learner more than I am a book scholar. I've learned my most important lessons not in a classroom, but in "the streets," and I don't mean that in a gangsta sense.

I did know one thing about God. Most of the people that regularly talked about him always seemed to have the same leather-bound ancient manuscript in hand—the Holy Bible. I knew I had a Bible buried in the bottom of a box somewhere, so I did some digging and finally unearthed it. Mine had a very feminine red cover, so I didn't use it as a fashion accessory, but I did open it up from time to time. I couldn't afford any classes, but on occasion I could afford a few minutes here and there to crack that dusty Bible open, hoping to shed some light on the mysteries of God.

What greeted me when I opened the cover of that book was exactly what I expected—confusion and boredom. The history was dry, the poetry didn't rhyme, and the doctrine was miles over my head. Yet my hunger for something beyond the drugs and depression compelled me to continue, irregularly dedicating time here and there to Bible reading. Finally I stumbled across some short, concise sections that spoke to me—the biblical proverbs. I began to dedicate my allotted Bible-reading time to the proverbs.

One day, I read a proverb that said, "Wisdom is before [in front of] him that hath understanding; but the eyes of a fool are in the ends of the earth" (Proverbs 17:24). The old English style always created an additional level of complexity, but I was getting used to it (and other easier-to-read translations do exist). This particular proverb struck a chord, and I pondered the possible meaning.

The first thing I thought about when anyone said the word "education" was schooling, classes, books, and so on. I knew I needed some God education, so my mind quickly shifted to the scholastic side. As a result, I was quickly daunted because book smarts were not my specialty. But this proverb shines a different light on education—or getting wisdom. It says if I have a level of understanding, I can see that wisdom is available right in front of my face. If I am smart, I can learn right where I'm at, as opposed to seeking out classes or studying abroad. And don't get me wrong, there is great merit in schooling, but a proper mentality about education allows a person to learn from whatever circumstances he is in—classroom or street. It is foolish to believe that a person cannot develop wisdom right where he is.

For a guy with limited resources, understanding this verse came as a great relief. I still recognized the value of education and eventually would take some Bible classes, but to realize that I could learn right where I was refreshed me. It makes sense from a non-biblical perspective, even to novice researcher like me. The person who understands this concept knows that he can learn wherever he may be in life. What's more, the verse suggests my preferred learning technique: learning by example. My nose might be in a book for a small portion of the day, and there is wisdom to be gained there. But most of the time I am living life; life is moving along before my eyes. What I see, what I do, and what I experience are all opportunities to learn, just so long as I don't look past them. Wisdom is right in front of me.

Years later, I took up the personal project of writing what I had learned about God, which is the content of this book. And as I was trying to group my thoughts, I knew there was a bunch of theory and reasoning and history to be explained—"book smarts." I also knew I didn't want my own book to put me to sleep. I began reflecting on that proverb about wisdom. I needed to put my discoveries into a context that would help them make sense. They needed to be understandable and applicable. I needed an awesome example to use.

So, applying that proverb, I started looking right in front of my face for wisdom. And you know, there it was. Sitting in the middle of the living room in my small apartment, chewing on a bone, was all the wisdom I would need to put my thoughts together.

Her name is Jenna. She's a yellow Labrador retriever, though her fur is almost completely white, with a little tan coloring around her ears and down her back. At 105 pounds, she has a large frame but is also a couple pounds overweight. Perhaps a couple plus. Her tail is like a thick, rolled-up hand towel, whipping items off shelves and coffee tables with no regard. She is a very good-natured dog, as her active tail indicates. My wife, Danielle, happens to be an animal lover, so before we even started dating, she already had Jenna tucked away at her apartment. When I got down on my knee to ask Danielle to marry me, I might as well have proposed to the dog too because they were a package deal. Regardless, I now love to be "Daddy" to Jenna.

Yep, that's right. I'm going to use my silly yellow Lab to bring out some deep truths about God. Jenna is right in front of me, right in my face, many hours in a typical day. In fact, she's *more* in my face than I sometimes like. There must be some wisdom, some education, to be gained from her. So where do we begin?

What Jenna provides initially is an epiphany in the area of coexistence. Obviously, Jenna is a dog. Equally obvious is the fact that I'm a human. Jenna can't do most of the things I can do; she can't talk or write or even use a toilet (an ability that I pride myself on). She's far less intelligent individually and as a species. Even the top-caliber, best-trained canines in the world, all put together, could never operate a computer keyboard or perform surgery. Job security for programmers and doctors, if the dogs ever take over. Anyway, a dog's capacity is so much less than ours that the two can hardly be compared. Jenna only understands the tiniest fraction of what I understand about life. And she will never be much smarter than that. Compared to me, my dog is grossly ignorant.

But here's the amazing part: Jenna and I live under the same roof. We coexist. Somehow, despite the incredible intelligence gap between humans and dogs, Jenna and I can live together, play together, and even communicate with each other. Jenna and I have reached an unspoken agreement. I take care of everything she needs: hundreds of dollars a year in food, bathroom trips in the bitter cold, pricey vet bills, and so much more. And in return she makes me smile. I don't know how, but that deal is totally worth it. You pet owners know what I mean.

In much the same way, I coexist on this planet with God. I don't entirely understand it, but he has chosen to live with a relatively helpless band of people known as the human race. Compared to him we're grossly ignorant, some grosser than others, yet he likes to keep us around. And he probably takes care of us more than we realize. He might even be willing to sacrifice for our benefit, which we will discuss later. And while we can't grasp everything, there is most certainly a small fraction that we can understand. This book is my small fraction.

God is above me, though I sometimes forget it. I am above Jenna, though she can be forgetful too. But these days, when I look at Jenna, she helps me to remember. She helps me to figure out this whole coexistence thing just a little better. And she's going to help me illustrate it too. She shows me that wisdom is everywhere, if our eyes are open.

> Wisdom is before him that hath understanding; but the eyes of a fool are in the ends of the earth.
>
> Proverbs 17:24 (KJV)

The Blonde Bulldozer

I remember my introduction to the oddball dog Jenna. I first had the pleasure of meeting a beautiful, wonderful girl named Danielle, now my wife, at my place of employment. Danielle and I began talking at a co-worker event—bowling night. After that we went on a few dates and sparks flew, as they say. As we grew closer, I inevitably went over to her apartment for the first time to hang out. I thought it would be just me and her. I was sadly mistaken.

My love interest met me at the door, but she didn't fling it wide open invitingly. Instead she opened it about a foot and stood in the gap. It seemed she was hiding something behind her. I could see what looked like a blonde head moving around rather sporadically a couple feet off the ground, and I heard a few light, snorting noises, but I couldn't make out what it was. Did she have something she wasn't telling me?

"Are you ready?" she asked with a smile on her face.

"Um, I guess…" I replied uncertainly.

She opened the door just far enough for the massive beast behind her to get a little leverage. To my horror, it scooted its way between her legs and the door, and was bearing down on me in seconds. I recognized it as a big, light-yellow dog, some kind of retriever, though it was larger than any I had seen before. Its energy was probably the most frightening thing. Once it was released from behind the door, this dog's mission could not be stopped. I stepped back, hoping that its mission was not my jugular.

"Meet Jenna!" my hostess said enthusiastically.

Fortunately for me, Jenna had a mission of only benevolence. Her goal was to show me affection with every fiber of her being—her bulldozer body, her slobber-loaded mouth, and her hair-emitting coat. I was dressed to impress Danielle, so I really didn't appreciate being bowled into, salivated on, and covered with hair. Still, how could I fault this animal for doing everything within her limited ability to show me her primitive form of love? As a natural reaction to her welcoming display, I reached down to pet her.

That evening, I gave my new buddy Jenna plenty of attention, but she gave me more. She wouldn't leave me alone. She was constantly sticking her snout under my hand or her big head in front of the TV. Danielle and I eventually had to shut her in the bedroom so we could watch our movie in peace. Moderate peace. Jenna whined a little. But from those simple beginnings came a new chapter of my life. It wasn't long before that wonderful woman and her dog became my family.

Jenna welcomed me before I even set foot in the door on that first day. And her welcoming ability continues to be dynamite today. Every time I come home from work, there she is, enthusiastic as she possibly can be. Every time she tries to bowl me and my wife over with her affection. And I love it every time. Jenna is so happy that I am a part of her life that she cannot contain herself. And her enthusiasm is contagious. Because she is so overjoyed to see me, I can't help but be excited to see her. I can't help but provide her the attention she craves.

When I first began to search out God, my motivation was to get his attention, assuming he really was up there. I couldn't solve the depression in my life, but I figured if anyone could, it was God. My main problem was that I had no idea how exactly to get a hold of him. He wasn't in the phone book, and I was fairly certain he didn't have a home address in Michigan. What could I do so that God would come down and fix up my life?

So I started sniffing around. I started trying to figure out if God really existed at all. My first source was the American populace. I valued social consensus quite a bit back then. As I began to look to the masses, I realized that this sniffing stage is where a great many people stagnate for their entire lives. Few had anything more than my vague undeveloped theories on God. Many people kind of believe there is something out there, but whether it is God or Buddha or Zeus remains unclear. Here in America, we typically choose "God" as the default supreme being that's somewhere out in space. So those in my immediate environment quickly chimed in with, "Sure, I believe in God." Not many went any farther than that.

But I wanted to go farther. I didn't want to sit in one place for my seventy years on this planet, mainly because where I was sitting then was pretty dismal. But before I could even really tackle God's existence as a legitimate possibility, I had to decide if the pursuit was worth it. Life is too full to pack in activities that are not beneficial, so I began to analyze the possibilities.

The best-case scenario was that God did exist and that he could drop something good into my life. This scenario provided some great benefits; who wouldn't want to be on the receiving end of God's positive attention? The worst-case scenario was that God didn't exist at all and that any pursuit of him was time wasted. But if he didn't exist, my primary purpose in life would become coping with the fact that I would inevitably die. In other words, if the best I could be in one hundred years is just a corpse, then *all* pursuits would be time wasted. It really wasn't a tough decision. I wasn't even sure God existed, but I decided that finding out would be worth it.

After pondering for a brief period, I made the decision that I would make God one of my pursuits. Somewhere in my brain

I flipped a switch to officially begin the searching process. But after flipping that switch, I immediately encountered the timeless dilemma that debilitates so many searchers: What do I do now? What action should I take?

To answer this question, I call upon my Blonde Bulldozer, Jenna. Jenna is obviously not versed in standard human greetings. She did not prance out the door and shake my hand heartily and say, "Pleased to meet you, sir." I would be silly to expect such a thing from an animal. I know Jenna is a dog, and she does dog things. She doesn't do human things very well at all.

You see, when Jenna barreled out from behind that door to greet me, I saw two things. Initially I saw a big, intrusive, uncontrollable hound racing toward me. But when I looked a little deeper, I saw a silly puppy that wanted my attention and affection more than anything on earth at that moment. I saw loving, hospitable intentions housed inside her foreboding 105-pound frame. So I forgave her for being a dog and offered to her the affection she desired because I could see that her heart was pure. My heart gave me no choice other than to reach down and pet the silly pup. Jenna got exactly what she wanted from me—all because she decided to take action.

So back to our question: What action do I take to try to find God? *Anything*, so long as it isn't *nothing*! Just make a move! I had been doing nothing in my life, and I was getting nothing back. But that silly dog got *something* from me—a loving response. Her motive won out over her physical action. I have to trust that God can figure out my motives as well as I can figure out Jenna's. And, like me, God appreciates our sincere desire to get closer to him more than any physical gesture. If God is going to reward any action, it is an action done out of sincere desire for him.

When Jenna first saw me, she had some options. She could have bitten me. She could have peed on my shoes. She could have turned tail and run the other direction. While these are also actions, what they would have shown was that Jenna's heart (or at least her brain) was not sincerely invested in connecting. They would have shown that she was not ready or capable of building a connection with me at that point. And as a result, our relationship would have been strained from day one. Our development would have been retarded.

But Jenna knew better. She chose a greeting that made me feel welcome. She had no clue what would develop from that first meeting—that I would one day be her provider, her play-buddy, and even her "Daddy." She did the only thing she knew she could and should do—she took action. I am so glad she did.

We, as humans, might say that we don't know if God exists, and we don't know what he wants us to do. We can float around in this mindset for as long as we like, but a connection with God is not just going to develop without some effort. I can't understand all the complex theological theories behind God. But most every human possesses the ability to make a move toward him. Any development we will see in any area of our lives will require some sort of action. The pursuit of God is exactly the same.

God knows we are humans, and therefore we do human things. For that reason, God has provided a number of human things we can do to express our sincere effort to draw closer to him. We can read books about him or read the Bible. We can see what a local church might say about him. We can help others who are less fortunate. But we cannot just sit on our butts or run away or oppose his ideas and expect our lives to get any better. God has given us an opportunity, not a requirement, to work with him in constructing the best possible life we can have. But we must be willing to cooperate.

I didn't know for sure if God existed. But if he did exist, I knew he would be the one (possibly the only one) capable of making my life better. So I threw out the welcome mat. I took a few steps toward him with sporadic church attendance, Bible reading, and prayer. If God did exist, I was determined to find out. And I was willing to work with him if he happened to show up. My actions were my proof.

God did show up in my life, but not exactly as I had planned. The religious knowledge I eventually developed helped, but the biggest advancements always came when I took action. The key to remember is that we don't get anything if we don't act. If we want God to reach down and give us attention in a way we can understand, we must first wander over toward him. Who knows what wonderful things are possible in our lives if we take the first step?

> Faith without works is useless.
>
> James 2:20b (NASB)

Part I:

God's Existence and Attributes: The Laws of Nature

Jenna's Guillotine

I had said, "I believe in God" on many occasions before I was ever seriously considering his existence. At the same time, I never connected any of my actions with this statement. A debate student is often assigned a view they do not necessarily believe, and yet they must debate. I don't know if it was my parents' church roots or a feeling of internal obligation, but I felt I had been assigned the God-exists view when the debate arose. It didn't mean that I *lived* like God existed or even knew how.

But when I added action—switched my search for God to active instead of passive—I made a smidgen of necessary headway. My church attendance, for example, proved that I had decided that I would be interested in perhaps following God, *if* he existed. Unfortunately, that if is one of the biggest ifs in human history. Wars have been fought over that if. Millions have died over that if. How on earth would I ever figure out if God existed?

As you have already noticed, I am big on practical application. This is the key reason God didn't get a whole lot of consideration from me in my partying college and post-college years. I couldn't see how some big, nebulous being had anything to do with my day-to-day life. I seemed to be doing a great job of balancing my job responsibilities and my rebellious drug use. I was doing okay whether God existed or not. So why would I change anything? If he showed up, I would cooperate, but I was pretty sure he wasn't going to show up.

Well, God didn't show up in the way that I thought he would. Instead, what did show up was a bunch of problems in my life. Consequently—or perhaps divinely—my life took an unpredictable turn for the worse: I got in a pretty bad rollover accident, totaling my truck. Things went smoothly for a little while after that, but then another downturn: my girlfriend CJ was taken to the hospital for a drug overdose. Then I got drug charges. Then CJ left me. Then the police raided my apartment for the second time. One bad thing after another skewered my life, and I was eventually forced to wonder if good things even happened anymore. Where was this God fellow I had heard so much about?

I started thinking that I was the most unlucky guy on earth. I thought life was really out to get me, and it wasn't fair. I felt I had been duped, tricked into thinking life was great when secretly it was a nightmare. I felt like I had been taken for a ride, and I wanted this ride to end. It was then that I began to think about ending it myself. Suicidal thoughts began to cloud my mind.

I was well aware that life's ride always ends in death. No one I knew had ever outsmarted their inevitable physical demise. The thought of this impending death weighed on me, like life's many other pressures. By my calculations, I had two possible ways to deal with death. I knew I couldn't stop it. I did have the option of abruptly giving in to it; suicide, the "easy way out." Or I had the option of futilely resisting it for the remainder of my days, coping. I figured this would take some heavy sedation, which I proceeded to administer through drugs and alcohol. I thought this was the only way to bear life's inevitable ride toward death—the worst ride ever.

Jenna's Ride

Let's step back from this dismal picture for just a minute. Life's ride is not necessarily a bad thing, as I had once concluded. Jenna loves going for rides. I remember one of the first times Jenna rode in my car. I was dating Danielle, and in the interest of advancing that relationship, I had put aside my concern about dog hair and let Jenna into my back seat. She was just a ball of energy bouncing around back there. Once we took off, Jenna had her head out the window, her ears and tongue flapping in the wind. It is a familiar picture for any dog owner. Jenna had been on many rides before, but they never seemed to get old for her.

Danielle and I began to talk, not really paying attention to Jenna. This was fine by her because she was on cloud nine with her open window and fresh air. But suddenly we heard a slight whimper and then a bunch of flailing and scratching on my seats. We looked back at her, wondering what silliness she was up to.

Well, it turned out that my car's interior setup is a little different than Danielle's back seat. On my door armrests the automatic window switch protrudes a little more than Jenna was accustomed to. So when we looked back at her, all we saw was her body. She had her head stuck in the window, and she was yanking and pulling with all her might to try to get loose. In order to get a better angle on all that fresh air, Jenna had put her paws up on the armrest, inadvertently pressing Up on the window switch. She nearly guillotined off her head when the window closed on her neck! I quickly let her loose from her self-made death trap with my driver-side switch. She was a little disoriented and a little leery of the window, but she was fine. Danielle and I had a good laugh at Jenna's expense, as we frequently do.

My Ride Continues

Back to my depressed state of being years earlier. At that time, I wondered how life had come to this. My childhood was a relatively happy one. Even when misfortune struck, I rebounded very quickly, as children can. In my teenage years, I waited anxiously as the prospect of independence unfolded before me. I looked forward to shedding the watchful confines of my parents' eyes. I was excited that I would finally be in the driver's seat in my life. But when the time came, independence was nothing like I had imagined. Jobs, finances, relationships, and circumstances in general, continued to throw me around. I was still in the back seat as life moved forward; I wasn't driving at all. The only thing I could predict about this ride was the inevitable conclusion: death. As my habits worsened, I could feel that suffocating death approaching fast. My past was past, my future was death, and the present just kept getting worse. Would I give up, or would I try to survive?

For some reason, I internally defaulted to "try to survive." Armed with this decision, I began to invest some effort into struggling free from my constricting circumstances. On the practical side, I tried to avoid parties and old friends and attempted to stay in closer contact with my family. On the spiritual side was the church attendance, Bible reading, and even some errant prayers to a God I wasn't sure existed. And slowly but surely, my life improved. The confining strength of my addictions lessened to the point that I was able to wriggle myself free. Though I still had mental and emotional baggage, death didn't seem to be so imminent in my life. I congratulated myself on a job well done.

In the wake of my moderate success, I was still left with a question as to why I happened to survive. Many people, especially those caught up in the addiction world, give in to suicidal thoughts. Others become consumed by their addictions. Still others are incarcerated continually or indefinitely. Yet I seemed to be at the exit stages of an alcohol- and drug-induced binge that had lasted for years. Sure, I had a voice inside me that said, "You can never beat these problems." But I also had a voice that told me that I could overcome, a voice that encouraged me through my struggles. I had chosen to listen to that voice. That voice gave me hope, and without hope, I would not have survived.

What a silly thing hope is. There is no measuring it. There is no explaining it in more than vague terms. And yet this invisible, unscientific element existed inside of me in an unknown quantity great enough to propel me to victory over my deadly vices. I'm sure that scientists could sit me down in a lab and poke and prod me for hours and never find physical evidence of the hope inside. But they don't have to find evidence because I know that hope is there. My evidence for hope is my survival. I know that hope came alive when I decided to have it. Who would want to live without hope?

This brings us back to the "big if"—God's existence. It had become quite clear to me that if I was in control, the best I could do was get into trouble. As Jenna's paw had played the key role in her window dilemma, so too had my hand played a key role in my suffocation. I had come to the conclusion that I was not in the driver's seat of life at all. So my question quickly became, who is in the driver's seat? Is there anyone in control?

I felt like I was at a horseracing track with a dollar to bet. There were only two horses in this heat: God Exists and Nothingness. Both had major cheering sections. If I bet on Nothingness, the best thing I could win was bragging rights while rotting in the ground. If I didn't bet, then I couldn't win anything. The only option with any payout whatsoever was betting God Exists. This option offers happiness and even possibly heaven. And the odds—well, different people will tell you different things. I may have listened to a couple spectators, but no one will truly know until the race is over and the betting is done. So when I had to make a final decision, I looked inside. And what did I find? I found hope.

Jenna might never understand that she was the one that had clamped her neck in the car window. It is even less likely that she will ever realize that I was the one who freed her. Like me, she probably congratulated herself for a well-played escape. Am I as ignorant as silly Jenna? Did I really think that the credit for my escape from my crushing addictions belonged to me? There is an undeniable connection between the time I spent living for myself and the "bad luck" I encountered. There is an equally undeniable connection between the "good luck" that resulted when I began my search for God. I chose to bet on God's existence, but I didn't do it blindly. I did it because the hope that pulled me through was not my own concoction; I can take no credit. The circumstances that helped me succeed were not controlled by me either. Both of these contributing factors came from a source outside of myself. That source is divine; that source is God.

The hope I discovered is definitely meant to encourage you, but the truth is that my story is not yours. Perhaps you need your own set of circumstances, your own divine assistance, to realize that God is real. But it is even more likely that you've already had this evidence in your life, whether or not you have recognized it as God's work. Wisdom is often directly in front of us, more obvious than we expect. After a great deal of puzzling, I found the evidence of God in my life. This is the evidence that makes me wonder. This is the evidence that makes me hope. This is the evidence that makes me believe.

> I would have despaired unless I had believed that I would see the goodness of the Lord in the land of the living.
>
> Psalms 27:13 (NASB)

Pound Puppies

I had reached the conclusion that God truly does exist, and I was interested in following up on his plan. This decision empowered me, but it hardly cleared my life of all the repercussions of my irresponsibility. My depression abated significantly, but addictions rarely just disappear. Drug charges don't just vanish. Breakups can leave anyone emotionally distraught. Often these intangible malefactors would team up against me, telling me that happiness was only a delusion. They tried to drag me down so that I would again embrace the deadly thoughts they contrived. Sometimes I could ward off these thoughts, and sometimes I could not.

In my endeavoring to rid myself of my internal enemies, I made an important discovery. The connection between my "God activities"—going to church, reading the Bible, and praying—and my staving off depression was apparent, but what I realized was *why* these positive actions were working (at least in the most practical sense). When I sat alone in my apartment, my focus was on my dismal state. My self-centeredness became a breeding ground for internal despair. But when I sat with others in an inspiring church service, suddenly my focus was directed away from myself, toward higher things. I was no longer confined by my sadness for at least the service duration. When I subtracted selfishness from my mindset, even in small bits, something good was deposited in my life in place of my depression. I was able to focus a little more on the truly good things in life. I was able to set my gaze upon the things of God.

I will admit that I was a bit concerned about this whole pursuit-of-God idea. My dad attended a very demonstrative church when I was younger, and to tell you the truth, I did not want to end up like some of the eccentric "crazies" in that church. They seemed a little *too* excited about this whole God thing. On the other side was my mom's traditional church, which didn't seem very excited at all. Her church mainly bored me. Really, I didn't want the commitment of a life of religiousness anyway. For the time being, I just wanted to take a spin around the block with God and see if it worked for me.

Jenna is a big fan of taking walks around the block, or the apartment complex, or the entire city of Lansing. She could walk forever, and she is fortunate to have two owners—me and my wife—who exercise her regularly. Not only that, but she has a roof over her head, medical benefits, and plenty of food and treats. It isn't doggy heaven, necessarily, but it works. Not all dogs have such a good home.

A good friend of mine used to work at the Humane Society, where there was no shortage of dogs. There was, however, a shortage of good homes willing to take in these dogs. Day after day he would feed the dogs and exercise them and clean up after them. When my friend and I hung out in the evenings, he would tell me about the various dogs that had arrived that day. Every now and then he would even bring an especially cute puppy home with him for a night to hang out with us. All my friends would bombard that dog with affection until he went back the next day.

Occasionally I would go to visit my friend during his shift. In fact, a lot of people visited the Humane Society, some to look for a pet, and some just to help out. At that time I didn't want a pet, but I certainly enjoyed taking the puppies for walks around the yard. I would look through the kennels and choose the cutest little dogs I could find for a few minutes of playtime. My friend, on the other hand, had job responsibilities. He did not have the luxury of choosing which dog he would walk. He had to take them all out during his shift. So I would be on one side of the property with a cute, perfectly behaved beagle puppy, and my friend would be on the other side, getting dragged around by a giant Rottweiler.

There was a monster difference between the beagle and the Rottweiler, besides just size. The beagle had cuteness going for him, but he also had the most important trait available in any pound: *adoptability*. This trait got my attention, and it got that puppy a spin around the yard with me. This trait also assured the puppy that it would not be long before he was adopted by a loving family.

Adoptability

If I wanted to better understand God, or go for a spin around the block with him, I needed to learn a lesson from that little beagle. I needed to become a little more adoptable. Like me, a dog is a self-centered animal. Food, water, and survival in general are at the top of most dogs' lists. I would be a fool to expect anything different, especially from a puppy. But what created that divide between the obnoxious Rottweiler and the adoptable beagle was just a smidgen of conscientiousness.

The Rottweiler at the Humane Society did what he wanted without a care in the world about the human on the other end of his leash. He didn't care about a connection or a relationship, and he also inadvertently bucked adoptability. Every bit of his attention was on himself.

The beagle puppy had just about the same mindset. When he got outside, he sniffed around and peed where he wanted and played how he wanted. He too was pretty selfish. But the difference was that while this little puppy was very focused on himself, he still had just a couple percentage points of his attention to give to me. He may have spent 98 percent of his attention on his own desires, but he was willing to spend the other 2 percent on me and what I wanted to do. He let me be involved in his life, and that made all the difference.

This is the key to adoptability, which is required for that much-needed spin around the yard with God. We have to take our eyes off ourselves—our victories and our defeats—for just a few minutes, and focus on God. I didn't expect the beagle to be perfectly behaved, nor did I expect him to come out of the kennel quoting Shakespeare. He was a dog, a young puppy, and I expected him to act accordingly. But I also required that if he was going to get a bunch of my attention, he had to give me just a little of his. I wasn't opposed to the Rottweiler just because he was a Rottweiler. There were plenty of larger or scruffier dogs at the Humane Society that did give me attention and got mine in return, just as Jenna had in our first meeting. I was opposed to the Rottweiler because he could not see me as anything more than an obstacle to his selfish desires. No relationship can develop, and no adoption can occur, until this attitude is changed.

A person shouldn't be expected to go to church one day and be a doctor of theology the next. Nor should he fear becoming a religious demonstrator from the eccentric churches. Getting connected to God is a step-by-step process, one day at a time. We still do human things a lot of the time, and God understands. He doesn't expect 100 percent of your attention the first time you think about him. But if you can drum up 2 percent, he is quite willing to take you for a spin and show you a thing or two.

If you can't drum up 2 percent, then you may be that big, disobedient Rottweiler. I know I was for a long time—doing my own thing. We certainly have the "right" to choose that route if we want. But there is a problem. That Rottweiler never grasped the fact that life was not all about him. My friend from the Humane Society often told the happy-go-lucky stories about the puppies, but there were other stories that were not so happy. Not every dog got adopted, and space at the Humane Society was not unlimited. Sometimes those dogs labeled *unadoptable* were dead dogs walking. The inevitable conclusion to their continual selfish displays was lethal injection.

Without even knowing it, the Rottweiler had made a choice. He never figured out that he was on death row. The workers dreaded having to end those dogs' lives, but at the same time, they could not allow entirely insubordinate dogs to consume valuable resources. The humans set the guidelines, but the dogs chose whether or not to follow them. By choosing to behave antisocially, those dogs chose by default to die. If the dogs could learn and develop, and could shift their attention away from themselves long enough to obey, they had a much better shot at adoption.

Take a Walk or Take a Hike?

I decided that I would prefer to give a few percentage points of my attention to God instead of assuming that the way I was going was just fine. I did not want to be the Rottweiler anymore; I wanted to live a better and longer life than that. I did not want to inadvertently sentence myself to death, or even a negative life. Like any normal guy, I wanted my life to be the best that it could possibly be. And I knew that in order for that to happen, I had to look toward God.

If we want to be adoptable to God, even to the extent of taking an occasional spin with him, then we have to understand a few things about him. The Rottweiler's biggest problem was that he didn't understand what I or the Humane Society workers wanted. The Rottweiler may have been thinking survival, but he was only seeing it within the confines of the doggy brain. He wasn't tying his survival to the most important factor in that survival—the human being. If we cannot tie the concept of a better life with the one who can make our lives better, we are yanking and pulling toward our graves.

So what can we understand about God? There must be some substance to him, or else we could never figure out how to attract his attention. There must be some certainties and definites, at least as they apply to our individual lives. For example, God cannot want me to both kick my brother in the stomach and not kick my brother in the stomach at the same time. Only one choice is possible. God has a preference for me in this situation. Following God's preferences is what makes our lives improve.

My brother's stomach seems like a minimal concern to a big God, which is why I chose to kick it (just kidding; my brother is a Marine, so I don't mess with him). Perhaps his stomach is a minimal concern, but the point remains that God by existing must have some things he prefers us to do or not do, especially if we have any intention of working with him. There are millions of different religious rules out there, and they can't all be right, nor can they all be wrong. There must be actions God prefers over other actions.

Going further, there must be a way that God truly is. He is painted in so many different lights by so many different religions and denominations. And although we will all undoubtedly be surprised in the end, some current views of God must be more accurate than others. Getting an accurate view of God is crucial to being able to please him, and to being adoptable by his standards.

Many people these days believe that there are many roads that lead to God. And although this is true in a personal sense—the sequence of my life is different from the sequence of yours—the statement cannot be true in a universal sense. God cannot prefer opposing things; one way must be most true. If one religion says God cares about humans and another says that he is indifferent, both cannot be right. God either cares, or he doesn't. It would be foolish to say he does both, which is exactly what the many-roads theology implies.

Here again, I have the "right" to choose any one of the many expressions of God. But my choosing a way does nothing to make that choice more or less true than the others. God's truth exists independent of man's whims or feelings. At the same time, God's truth is knowable, and in many cases obvious. For example, does God support or not support cold-blooded murder? He cannot both support and not support it. I would agree with most people that he does *not* support cold-blooded murder. General social consensus, my conscience, and basic religious ethics all agree with this statement. The point is that there are some things about God that we can logically ascertain.

Back when I made the decision to not be the Rottweiler, it would have been great if I could have gone right to God and had a fireside chat with him about his characteristics and policies. But I didn't figure the chances of that were very good. So much like my conclusion regarding murder, I turned to the same three sources. I looked first to society (social consensus), which had essentially been my primary guide through life to that point. Secondly, I looked inside myself (conscience) for what I had come to understand over the years. And thirdly, I skeptically turned to religious institutions (basic religious ethics) with the understanding that someone had to have a better idea than the others about what God truly was like. I also tried to incorporate balance because I understood the danger of following only society, or my feelings, or a church.

I knew God wanted something from me, but I wasn't sure what would get his attention. My only recourse, if I truly sought a connection with him, was to begin to focus a little less on myself and a little more on him. I did not want to be like that Rottweiler, so self-centered that he would die from it. I wanted to know the right way, the best way, through life. I wanted to know God.

> There is a way that seems right to a man, but in the end it leads to death.
>
> Proverbs 14:12 (NIV)

Light Years Ahead

Although God is an ultra-complex being, he still has some attributes that can be known and understood by humans. In order to begin to understand these attributes and get a better picture of what God wants from us, it is most typical to turn to one of three information sources, as mentioned in the previous chapter. The first is society and surroundings. The second is self, made up of internal thoughts and emotions. The third is various religious teachings and doctrine. Balance is very important in avoiding a skewed perception of God.

Society, the first source typically consulted, has set up a series of ranking systems that we live by. Hierarchy has always been a staple of any organized society. While most of us agree that "all men are created equal," we are still aware of the fact that *mayor* trumps *citizen*, and *governor* trumps *mayor*, and *president* trumps *governor*. And while this is a physical example of hierarchy, there are also some leadership qualities that trump others, according to society.

The most highly sought-after leadership quality as determined by society in general is *intelligence*. Smarts. By social estimation, you can't be a good leader unless you're a pretty smart person. No one wants to follow a dummy. Although there are multiple exceptions, for the most part people follow after intelligence. They trust people who have knowledge. They seek after wisdom. And intelligence is definitely a good thing.

So in looking at God's attributes, the first question that comes up for me, especially in qualifying him for a leadership role, is, how smart is God? Society and religion have a varicty of formulated answers to this question, and so does my internal logic. First off, I'm not going to blow anyone out of the water when I say God is smarter than me. That's very logical. I have already admitted how pathetically I had managed my own life, and I figured God could do exponentially better. If you have a problem you can't solve, you don't go to the village idiot. You go to someone who is smarter than you are.

Well, God is smarter than I am, and I hate to burst anyone's bubble, but he's smarter than you are too. In fact, it stands to reason that God is smarter than people in general, and smarter than the even smartest human out there. I don't see God being outsmarted by any man or woman here on earth. Plus I can't imagine a professor ever telling him, "Well, God, you got an A in theology, but you missed a few problems on the calculus exam." I'm pretty sure God knows everything we know collectively—he must be able to ace any one of our scholastic courses.

Taking it a step further, I don't think God was surprised when we discovered that the earth was round or that gravity held us down to the planet. It seems he knew all about the stuff we've discovered before we discovered it. He didn't shout, "Holy mackerel, I can't believe there's a vaccination available for smallpox." When *we* finally figured it out, he had known all along. Our discoveries are old news to him.

That means that there's probably a whole lot more that we haven't discovered that God already knows. The human race seems to be in a desperate scramble to figure out everything about this universe. We explore the outer regions of space. We dive to the depths of the oceans. We test, define, and manipulate nature's rules in laboratories across the globe. All this we do in search of information that we know exists. God has this information. Man is still discovering, but God already knows.

Perhaps our yellow Lab, Jenna, can help illustrate the intelligence gap between man and God. When Jenna first met me, she did not know a whole lot about me. But she did know one thing: she knew that I could do "magic." All I had to do was walk in a room, and suddenly brightness shined on Jenna and everything else. And when I walked back out, the brightness went with me. Sure, I wish I were talking about my thousand-watt smile, or maybe my intelligence, but I'm not that bright of a guy. I'm simply talking about my amazing ability to use a light switch.

To Jenna, when the lights come on, she has no capacity to figure out why. Jenna can definitely see the light; her squinting makes this obvious. She may even be able to associate the light with me, thinking, *Every time Daddy comes in, that bright thing comes on.* But aside from this very basic understanding, Jenna will never be able to understand how that light works.

I, on the other hand, *do* understand a lot more about how that light works. It really isn't very amazing at all. I understand that the switch completes an electrical circuit inside the wall, and nearly instantaneously, power is sent through that circuit, to which the light bulb is connected. The filament inside that bulb gets white hot, illuminating the room. Jenna will probably never even grasp that the switch has anything to do with the light, so she has no chance whatsoever of conceptualizing electricity. She just doesn't have the capacity.

Now I might think I'm smart because I can remember a little electricity trivia from seventh-grade science. We as humans might think we're smart because we have degrees or certificates or impressive experience. But the truth is that we can never truly grasp the inner workings of the universe; we can only scratch the surface. Our best understandings are like Jenna's knowledge of light. We have so much to learn but relatively so little capacity. One of our first mistakes is thinking that we are going to understand *everything* about God. He's just too deep for a human to comprehend fully. There will always be an element of God that remains magical or miraculous to us.

Now don't get me wrong; I am totally for learning and self-improvement and understanding God the best we can—these are the purposes of this book. This universe is incredibly vast, and even collectively mankind cannot fathom its depths. But that doesn't mean that the depths don't exist. If anyone has the key to those depths, it must be none other than God himself. It would be safe to say that God has every piece of information for which we are still searching. He knows everything there is to know about our universe.

Really, it can't be any less, or else God would be like Zeus or a "tree spirit" or any one of the intellectually limited mythical gods of ancient times. There's just no point in even having a god if he can't provide wisdom in *every* given human situation. It's like petitioning the mayor when only the governor can pardon you; there's no point. I wouldn't want to pray to a mayor god or governor god or vice-president god; I want to talk with the big cheese himself. The true God must be all knowing, or he isn't God.

I look at the world, and many times I see a jumbled, unsolvable mess. Most of us see the world like that from time to time. But this mess doesn't confuse or perplex God. He knows which switches control which lights and where the universe's energy flows from. Like Jenna, we aren't going to understand all these switches or be able to use them. From time to time we might even be "rudely" awakened from our naughtiness by the light, as Jenna is when she is caught sleeping on the couch. But if nothing else, we are going to figure out that God is smarter than we are. He knows the things we don't. He knows everything.

The first knowable attribute of God is that he is all knowing. This fact becomes crucial in our understanding of his characteristics. But let's not stop here. God is not one-dimensional, as he is sometimes portrayed. He really wouldn't do much good for us if he only had intelligence. There would be little benefit to pursuing him if he was just a big, nebulous blob of information, just like Jenna would have a hard time following me if I were only a brain. And like most people, I have always been into benefits. So let's figure out what God does with all this knowledge.

> "For my thoughts are completely different from yours," says the Lord. "And my ways are far beyond anything you could imagine."
>
> Isaiah 55:8 (NLT)

Power and Play

"Knowledge is power." Businessmen and executives tout this saying in affirming their leadership positions (at least in movies), and there is definitely some value to the quote. Certainly, we know that knowledge and power are not the same things; Webster makes that obvious. The definition of *knowledge* deals with facts learned and information, whereas the definition of *power* talks about ability to do or act. But there is a definite link between knowledge and power, which the saying implies. The ability to act—to exert power—is based in large part on the knowledge that a person possesses.

Jenna doesn't possess a whole lot of knowledge, but her understanding has improved over the years. It used to be that any item in her immediate vicinity was instantly dubbed "Jenna's toy." Flip-flops, seat belts, stuffed animals, and anything that came in contact with the pup felt the wrath of her chewing. As she grew, she came to understand that only certain items are hers to play with. Among these items is a retriever staple—the tennis ball. Her life is not complete without the trusty tennis ball in her mouth. She may not know much, but she knows that the tennis ball is hers!

I used to play with Jenna and her tennis ball a lot when I first met her. On one occasion I was playing fetch with Jenna inside the apartment, and the ball bounced into the bathroom. Jenna chased the ball in and didn't come back out for a minute. Then she poked her head out the bathroom door, with no ball in her mouth and a distressed look on her face, and then went back in. Then she came out, then went back in again. She repeated this several times until she finally piqued my curiosity. I followed the troubled pup back into the bathroom.

There, sitting in the bathtub, was Jenna's tennis ball. Not only had Jenna learned which toys were hers, but she had also come to understand that "bad things" happen to her in the bathtub. Mainly baths. So although she possessed the ability to climb into the tub, she wasn't going to risk it. But at the same time, she wasn't going to let her precious tennis ball, her prized toy, go without an effort.

I figured it would be a good test of deductive reasoning for the pooch, so I told her, "Get your ball." She looked and me, then looked at the ball, and stepped forward in action. She is just tall enough to get her neck over the side of the tub, so she bravely stuck her head in and stretched for the ball. She was getting close to reaching it when she realized that the edge of the tub was cutting off her air supply. With a wheeze she pulled her head back in dismay. She knew what she wanted: that precious seventy-nine-cent tennis ball. But she could not figure out for the life of her how to get it.

Mankind has a similar dilemma, at a little higher level. We are very informed, educated, and knowledgeable. This makes sense because information is one of our highest pursuits, collectively. So often we know what we want out of life, be it a tennis ball, a career in showbiz, or a relationship with God. The problem is that we don't know how to get there. We don't know what action to take to achieve our dreams, just like poor Jenna. We know what is wrong, but how to fix it eludes us.

We can see here that both the *what* and the *how* are knowable things. Both find their origins in knowledge. The *what* is sort of a basic, observational knowledge. The facts. The *how* is an additional piece of knowledge related to the application of those facts. The knowledge-is-power saying could actually be better stated, "*Properly applied* knowledge is power." Understanding the *how* is what gives the knower power. If you know *how* to do it, you can do anything.

Reflecting back on God's intelligence, we reached the conclusion that he knows everything. This would certainly include the *whats*, but it also includes the *hows*. God is not stumped by our dilemmas. He knows how to defeat any problem that we can ever encounter in our lives—addiction, sickness, depression. He has every cure. Because of his proper application of knowledge, God has the ability to do anything. Because he is all knowing, God is all powerful.

I know that God being all powerful makes sense to me, and of course it is a religious institution standard. But perhaps on this point we face the first minor refutation from society in general. Maybe they can accept *all knowing* as an attribute of God, but *all powerful* seems a bit too presumptuous in a world where bad things happen. I disagree. Bad things happened in my life because I was trying to run the show, not because God lacked power. I can't blame him for the failures and misery I had because I was not listening to his *what* or *how*. Society cannot discredit God's power simply because we have messed things up beyond our power to repair them. Our success, individually and as a society, depends on an all-powerful God. If there is a force that can outrank God's power, we are all in big trouble.

Like Jenna, each and every one of us will come face to face with the word *impossible*. Most of us already have. Jenna faced an impossible dilemma with the bathtub—one that she had no idea how to solve. She choked herself on the side of the tub over and over, glancing my way with each failure. Why did she keep looking toward me? Because her *impossible* was my *easy*. She recognized that I was the one who could end her struggle, which I did by reaching in and pulling out her favorite toy.

What are we going to do when we face the impossible? Will we give up on our situation or our hopes and dreams or our family just because it feels impossible? Or will we dig down to find the hope that reveals a God who is more powerful than any difficulty we encounter? God's power is not just some big, theological concept without any practical application to our lives. God's power is what we need to make it through life's impossibilities. Often it is the *only* thing that will work.

God wants us to discover who he is. At points in my exploration, I felt a little bit like I was reading a résumé. *Name: God.* Okay, you have my attention. *Special Skill 1: Knows everything.* That could be very useful; there's quite a bit I don't know yet. *Special Skill 2: Can do anything, including the impossible.* Now we're talking. I have many impossible things I need to overcome. This God seems to be exactly what I'm looking for. But there's a whole lot more to this résumé. I wonder what else he can do…

> For nothing is impossible with God.
>
> Luke 1:37 (NIV)

Jenna's Poop and God's Justice

God is all knowing. When it comes to the facts, God has them. God is all powerful. When it comes to abilities, God knows how to accomplish anything. But there is far more to life than just facts and abilities. Much of our lives is lived in a gray area not well defined by either of these two factors. We're just not sure what we want *or* how to get it.

We have a tendency to overvalue facts and abilities because they are the most easily measurable. They give us something to grasp. For instance, if I see a weight bench with a barbell on it, there are some very solid facts I can gather. Let's say it has three forty-five-pound plates on each side. That means that there is a total of 315 pounds on that bench, including the bar; that is a measurable fact. Also measurable is my ability to bench-press that amount; I can lift 315 pounds exactly zero times. Both the facts of the weight bench situation and my ability to affect it are easy to figure out.

But here's a gray-area question that isn't so easy to answer: Is 315 pounds heavy? I would say yes from my perspective as a weakling. But not everyone would agree. Many professional football players warm up with that weight. They would say that bench pressing 315 pounds is not heavy at all. Amateur weightlifters might say that 315 pounds is "kind of heavy." Different people would provide all different answers when asked if this amount of weight is heavy, from "impossibly heavy" to "heavy but obtainable" to "easy-pie lightweight." Everybody sees that 315 pounds from a little different perspective, though it is still the same amount of weight.

Hopefully no one in the weight room would ever get into a fight over who had the right perspective on the 315 pounds. If they did, the guy who said it was light would probably win. Really, in the big picture, nobody cares if you believe the weight is heavy or light. But there are far weightier matters that people argue about all the time—matters that have a lot more at stake. Take for example, capital punishment: Is it right or wrong to kill someone who has killed others? People debate this issue all the time in the legislatures, in the streets, and in the jury room. Everybody has a different view, and a man's life hangs in the balance. I think most of us can at least agree that this is a decision that should not be made lightly.

At the heart of the capital-punishment debate, as well as every other moral quandary, is the question, *Is it right or wrong?* This question may be the toughest we will ever face. The challenge of defining *right* and *wrong* is prevalent in every major controversy in history. Wars are fought over who is right and who is wrong. Nations split over who is right and who is wrong. Marriages fail as they try to hash out who is right and who is wrong. The debate alone has the power to destroy.

I've heard it said by some that right and wrong do not exist. When someone says that, my favorite response is to punch them over and over in the arm. Hopefully it isn't the guy who thought 315 pounds was light. The goal is not to beat them into submission but simply to show that one way feels right, and one way feels wrong. Getting punched repetitively feels painful. It feels wrong, at least to the punch receiver. This illustration is not meant to condone following only our feelings but simply to show that it is obvious even to our most basic sensory device, the physical body, that right and wrong exist.

So *who* is right and *who* is wrong? The answer is simple: if I'm in a debate with you, I'm right and you're wrong. Not really; this is just the typical human answer to that question. This answer displays the incredible difficulty we have admitting that we are not right (in other words, *wrong*). Even if someone is verifiably smarter than we are, we still have a tough time admitting we are wrong. Even when someone is physically superior to us, we have a hard time backing down. We often defy logic just to stick to our guns, blinded by our own sense of rightness. But if we are smart, we will realize that we are not always right.

For a long time after I met Jenna, it was just fun and games. I would play with her and give her treats and basically do all the enjoyable dog stuff. It was all good. But there came a day when Jenna and I had a little disagreement over what was wrong and what was right.

Jenna's position was that she had eaten a lot of food that day, and her digestive tract eventually let her know that she had exceeded her daily storage limit. She had therefore decided that it was appropriate to release said excess amounts of food. Of course, she didn't articulate her viewpoint quite so well; she just opened her bowels and crapped all over the carpet in the living room while Danielle and I were away. Point taken.

I, on the other hand, disagreed quite vehemently with Jenna's approach. When I walked into the apartment and the stifling aroma of feces struck my nostrils, I knew one thing for certain—something was *wrong*. "Jenna!" I angrily exclaimed. I smacked her on the head a couple times and sent her to her sulk spot under the kitchen table. There she stayed, being careful not to make eye contact with me while I cleaned up her mess.

Jenna has a natural inclination to poop in a particular spot. That spot is *wherever she happens to be when she gets the message from her digestive tract*. Inside or outside, it doesn't matter to her. The world is her toilet. The only problem with this is that *I* do not so much appreciate poop in my apartment. In fact, I have instituted a no-poop policy for Jenna while inside, as have most other dog owners. Any violation of this policy must be severely reprimanded.

Why have I come up with this policy? It goes back to coexistence. If Jenna had her way, we would be living in a dog-manure storage unit. I cannot live under those conditions. So in order to allow me and Jenna to live together, I have determined in this case what is right and what is wrong for her. And dog poop on the carpet is *so* wrong.

Humans turn to a lot of sources when determining what is right and wrong. We listen to social consensus. We rely on our own logic. We ask our priests or pastors. But ultimately we are most likely to determine what is right and wrong ("for us") by listening to our feelings. Society largely encourages this personal interpretation of the ambiguous "right" and "wrong." "You've got to follow your heart, do what's right for you," seems to be the reasoning. And while there's some truth to this, we must understand that our reasoning and feelings are not always right. Most of us would be criminals if we only did what we felt like doing.

Right and wrong do exist; we've already addressed that. But in order to understand what they are—where the lines are drawn—we cannot turn internally. We must look to a more intelligent, more powerful source. We find good guidelines in the laws of social authorities and governments; laws against murder, stealing, rape, and so on. And certainly God approves of these particular rules. But if we want to make the ultimate determination between right and wrong, especially on more questionable, gray-area issues, we must turn to the ultimate authority.

God is the one who gets to decide what is right and what is wrong. We cannot expect a peaceful coexistence with God if we ignore his living parameters. He doesn't want his house filled with crap any more than I want my apartment filled with it. It is great to be able to coexist—to have a connection—with God, but certainly we have the choice of rejecting his rules. Jenna's life greatly improves when she accepts my rules, and our lives will improve greatly when we decide to accept God's rules. If God does not supersede feelings in our lives, we are not truly cooperating with him.

So here's where the challenging part comes in: admitting that we are wrong. Like Jenna, we all have some areas we crap up from time to time. This internal pull, our human nature, can feel so right, but it isn't always. We have to be willing to elevate God to a level that outranks our opinions and feelings. Jenna and I face some monster communication gaps, but even she can figure out what I don't like. I make my displeasure obvious to her. And many times God's displeasure is obvious as well.

Right and wrong exist, and they have an author. That author is not human emotion because human emotion can be volatile and downright erroneous. That author is not human logic because we don't know everything; many times we can't see the whole picture. God is the author of what is right and wrong. If we do not agree with this, we are degrading God's authority and intelligence. We do not know better than God under any circumstance. To believe we do is dangerous. Our best bet is to cooperate with his standards.

This early step—designating God as the determiner of right and wrong—does not mean we always know what his determinations are. Again, gray area abounds, and the debates down here on planet earth continue. Throughout history, people and organizations have done some very misguided things under the guise of "godly command." But whatever they have done does not change the deep truth that only God determines what is right and wrong.

God knows humanity is in need of some housebreaking. He is aware that we get confused about his standards and what is truly right and wrong. But unless we work with him and perform that excruciating task of admitting that we are wrong sometimes, we are going to have a hard time peacefully coexisting with him. We might have to change and leave our poopy habits behind. God's standards are high, but the payout of a positive connection is well worth it. We can't be perfect, but everyone can try to improve.

Life gets a whole lot better when we let the expert, God himself, determine what is right and wrong for us.

> All of us have strayed away like sheep. We have left God's paths to follow our own.
>
> Isaiah 53:6a (NLT)

Part 2:

God and Mankind: The Laws of the Land

God the President

When my wife and I were apartment shopping, our choices were reduced significantly by the fact that we had Jenna in tow. We had to choose a pet-friendly complex, mainly because it is very difficult to keep a 105-pound Lab like Jenna hidden. And while this pet-friendly area is a little more expensive for us, Jenna loves our apartment complex. Why? Because many other residents also have dogs, so Jenna gets to see a lot of fellow canines when she goes outside. She is always meeting new friends, and for me it is entertaining to see the chemistry she has with other dogs.

One day Jenna met a new friend named Oscar. Oscar is a miniature dachshund, also known as a wiener dog. His fur is black with brown edging, and he probably weighs about seven pounds—almost one hundred pounds less than Jenna. Oscar was still a puppy when Jenna met him, so he basically looked like a little hamster on a leash.

When Jenna first saw Oscar, she was instantly intrigued. In her excitement, Jenna tugged furiously on her leash to get closer to him, and it was all I could do to hold her back. I think she thought he was maybe a squirrel or something, and she was getting ready to get her chase on.

Oscar's reaction was a little different. The initial look on his face was "Holy crap, I can't believe they make dogs that big!" He cowered behind his owner but eventually ventured out to see what this behemoth could possibly be.

Slowly but surely I let Jenna have a little more leash so she could get closer to Oscar, and Oscar's owner did the same. Their noses connected, and there was a lot of excited sniffing and snorting. Oscar ran back to his owner in excitement. Then he came back to Jenna. Jenna did a lap around me in excitement, and returned to Oscar. In a few minutes, the two dogs got comfortable enough that we could let them occupy the same space. We stopped holding them back.

The frenzied smellings continued for the dogs, this time extending to more than just sniffing each others' snouts. And then suddenly Oscar realized what was going on. Jenna was no longer confined by the leash, so Oscar wasn't protected by the ability to run outside of her range. In other words, Oscar was in Jenna's world now. As soon as he figured this out, he rolled over on his back as if to say, "Well, if you're going to eat me, just get it over with."

I'd say that was a pretty smart thing for Oscar to do. He was the male in this little meeting, but he wisely conceded the position of "alpha male" to his female superior. When he saw Jenna's dominance in size alone, he wisely submitted to her. Fortunately for Oscar, Jenna couldn't figure out how to eat him, so everything worked out all right. Both dogs gained a new friend.

We've looked at God's intelligence, power, and judgment (between right and wrong). In all three cases, he well outranks mankind—a well-known fact. He is the one best suited to distinguish what is right and wrong for mankind.

And then there's me. I outrank God in ignorance, weakness, and foolishness, among other inferior traits. Yet somehow, in many cases, I seem to value my own opinion above God's. Chalk that one up to my foolishness. This is why it is so critical to be able to admit when we are wrong especially in comparing what we think and what God thinks. If there is a conflict of opinion between God and me, I'll give you one guess who is right.

As we see from the meeting between Oscar and Jenna, there is something natural that should happen when an inferior meets a superior. There might be some sniffing, much of which we've done in previous chapters, to determine who the superior truly is. There might be some investigation, some realization, and maybe even some excitation as we begin to figure things out. But as with Jenna and Oscar, the superior in *our* lives quickly becomes quite obvious. In every way, we are the inferiors, and God is the superior. We have to understand our role before we can properly act on it.

An Appropriate Reaction

Jenna may be the "alpha male" when it comes to many of the smaller dogs in our apartment complex. I've seen many of these dogs pull a routine similar to Oscar's, rolling on their backs, bellies exposed, hoping to see the light of day again. As I mentioned, I find it quite amusing to watch the inter-dog chemistry at work. But this alpha-male concept applies to more than just her doggy buddies. It applies to our human-and-dog family unit as well.

In our apartment, I am the alpha male. My wife might sometimes disagree on that, but that's a whole different book. Right now I'm just talking about Jenna and me. I don't really mind if Jenna ranks above or below the other dogs in the complex. What I care about is that she knows with utmost certainty that she is below *me*—that she submits. She might not be able to speak English, but when it comes to submission, actions speak louder than words.

So how does Jenna act out her submission? How do I know she submits? Well, first of all, she makes an effort to obey my commands and rules. In the normal course of life, this level of submission is fine most of the time. But every now and then Jenna really messes up, like a misguided pile of turds on the apartment floor. This is when her submission is really tested. When I come home and find her major screw ups, I make my displeasure obvious. Jenna is then left with an important choice.

When we do something contrary to God's rules and realize it, our reaction is everything. We can make excuses. We can deny the error altogether. We can attack the regulation, which is indirectly an attack on God's judgment. Or we can do the right thing and submit to God's authority by admitting our mistake and attempting to do better. God isn't going to force us to feel guilty or fall down on our knees in repentance. He's just hoping that we are smart enough to do so on our own.

Jenna normally chooses to do the right thing when she messes up. She submits to my authority. She gets smacked (lightly), she gets scolded, and she has a time out while I clean up her poo. But a few minutes later everything is all right. We are back to playing and wrestling around like we always do. For humans, admitting that we are wrong is one of the hardest things to do, but it is ultimately one of the most rewarding as well. God cannot work effectively with us if we refuse to admit our mistakes. We cannot build our connection with him if we do not accept our subordinate role—no matter who we are.

A Submissive King

Even people in the highest authoritative positions are wise to submit to God. The Bible boasts of King David and the wonderful things he did. This is the same David from the classic story of David and Goliath. He grew up an honorable man, strong in battle, and was eventually crowned king of the ancient nation of Israel. He is even called "a man after [God's] own heart" (Acts 13:22, NIV). But he wasn't perfect by any means. In one instance, probably his worst lapse, he ogled one of his loyal subjects' wives, and eventually ended up sleeping with her. Next, to conceal his blunder, David arranged for that loyal subject to be killed so David could marry the subject's wife (2 Samuel 11). Now how on earth does a man this conniving get such a great reputation as being a man close to God?

The answer is simple: when David realized his mistake, he sincerely submitted to God's authority. He didn't turn away from God or make excuses. He simply admitted, "I have sinned against the Lord" (2 Samuel 12:13, NASB). God doesn't expect perfection out of humankind right off the bat. We can build our connection with him despite our imperfections. But unless we submit to his authority, especially under the duress of our screw ups, we cannot coexist peaceably with him. We cannot expect a beneficial relationship if we cannot accept our inferiority to God.

The Risk and Reward of Authority

Like ancient Israel, America is a nation built on a system of authority. In fact, every organized nation throughout history has been built on some variety of an authoritative system. Right and wrong are sometimes difficult to define. But without definitions we have no structure, and without structure we have no country. Having a government is risky business because it requires you to trust the system to some degree. But a governmental system is absolutely imperative if development is going to occur. Authority is foundational to society's advancement.

When we look at America, we see the result of a lengthy history of authoritative development and the prosperity it has provided us. Most of us submit to such a top-quality system. We pay our taxes, we don't kill each other, and we drive a certain speed all because we believe in and submit to the governmental system (obviously, with some exceptions). And as a result, our living system flourishes.

There are some risks to "electing" God as a personal authority—to president of my life. The main risk is that he may implement some policies and regulations that I do not like. His ways might not seem right or feel right to a limited human being's senses. But the problem is that if my senses or intuitions outrank God, then I truly have not accepted his authority. I am shunning the very foundation of the connection with him. Chaos is sure to result.

You see, there is a reason that I do not have a pet tiger or giant squid or gazelle. Sure, I may have the resources to give these animals good lives, but the problem has nothing to do with me. The problem is that these animals would not submit to my authority over them. They would destroy the apartment and probably attack me and my wife in the process. As a result of their inability to submit, these animals are unadoptable to me. We cannot coexist. It does not matter what wonderful abilities and intentions I may have if they are unwilling to cooperate by heeding my authority.

Making God the president of my life is an important step toward the benefits he has for us. It begins our development, and it is entirely in our hands. Accepting God's authority takes him out of the realm of "theology" and applies him practically to our situation. We may not know what exactly God wants from us, but giving him authority means that we are going to try to understand and follow his rules. And when we fail, as we inevitably will, we must be willing to do one of the hardest things known to man: admit our faults and change. When we approach God with this submissive viewpoint, we are setting ourselves up to strengthen our connection with the most intelligent, most powerful, most just being in the universe. It is very good to be on his side. It is foolish not to be. The choice is ours.

> Submit yourselves therefore to God.
>
> James 4:7a (KJV)

Moments of Truth

One morning, Herman the goldfish woke up with no idea that this day was going to be different. Herman was a happy resident of the small fishbowl that sat on the cabinet in our apartment. There he and his roommate Eclipse the betta fish spent their days swimming around and watching the big world outside of their transparent home. They waited with anticipation for their daily feeding from the big, upright, two-legged monsters. They eyed with concern the four-legged monster that prowled the floor. So far there had been no incident.

This day would be an exception. Herman swam his morning and afternoon laps as normal. Then he noticed something frightening. The four-legged monster was just sitting there, staring at the fishbowl. The two-legged monsters were nowhere to be seen. Herman's heart raced as he glanced over toward the four-legged monster's food and water dishes. Both were empty. *Oh, no!* he thought.

And just like that, the four-legged monster had her front paws on the cabinet. Her disgusting tongue was splashing around at the top of the fishbowl until the unthinkable happened—the whole bowl went over. Water poured from the top of the fishbowl, and Herman couldn't hang on. He flopped out onto the apartment floor.

This is it, he thought as he flopped around on the tile. His movement brought the attention of the four-legged monster, and she sniffed him over to try to determine his edibility. He decided to play dead; he didn't have much energy left anyway. Soon he didn't have to fake any more as his consciousness faded. It was about then that I walked in the apartment door.

"Jenna!" I exclaimed. I rushed to the scene of the crime. Jenna slunk away, knowing she had been naughty. I righted the fishbowl, which contained about a third of the original water and a terrified betta fish. I scooped up a near-dead Herman and placed him in the bowl, where he began to float upside down. I tried the help him stay upright, and Eclipse worked to provide moral support. Though I thought he was a goner, he slowly came around and started swimming on his own. He had survived the horrors of life outside the fishbowl.

What Danielle and I provide for our pets is, first and foremost, an environment in which they can survive. It wouldn't do much good for Herman if I brought him home from the pet store and dumped him out on the couch. He wouldn't survive without a water bowl in which to live. Jenna wouldn't survive without daily food and water. Before any regular interaction can occur between me and my pets, I must first be able to maintain them.

When we look at God in a presidential role, maintenance is usually the first thing we desire. Of course, we aren't generally talking about bare necessities. When I run out of milk, for example, I do not start praying for God to magically refill my milk jug. Nor do I call the White House and ask the president to send milk immediately. What I expect from the president of the United States is that he maintains the country in which we live—so that *I* have the ability to go buy my own milk. In the bigger picture, I am initially looking to God to maintain the world I live in. I want him to watch out for the big things in my life while I take responsibility for those I deem little. I remember all too well what happens when I try to take control, and humanity doesn't have that great of a track record either. I am happy to let God be in charge of maintenance.

So what does God do in his presidential role? We see the president of the United States nearly every day in the news, but God is not so visible. Keeping in mind that he is all knowing, it is quite clear that maintenance of human begins is well within his skill set. Therefore he knows exactly what we need to survive and thrive collectively and individually. While we may be confused about needs and wants, God knows that oftentimes what we need is simply a *defining moment.*

Defining Moments

Basketball is my favorite sport, and it is a wonderful illustration of defining moments. The goal is obviously to have the most points when the game is over. But the game itself is far more than just tallying points. The scoring doesn't move consistently. One team may score ten points in a row. One team may miss ten shots in a row. It might even be the same team at different times in the game. There are scoring runs and scoring droughts. The team that has the strongest scoring runs usually ends up as the winner.

So how might a team go on a scoring run? Well, if you dissect the game even further, there are key plays that trigger scoring runs. If a player makes a big shot or a strong defensive play, momentum has a tendency to shift. Often the scoring runs can be traced back to one of these big, momentum-shifting plays. These are the plays that make the highlight reels. They are watched over and over in slow motion. And if you look carefully, you can sometimes see that the defender's fingers were centimeters away from blocking the shot. That shot went through the hoop and started a scoring run. That scoring run changed the game. As a result, that defender's team went home losers. The difference between winning and losing was only a few centimeters. This play was one of the game's *defining moments.*

This is how God works in our lives. He knows that if you control the defining moments, you control the entire course of the game. So he does just that; he controls the defining moments. Instead of stepping out onto the floor and abolishing the team he dislikes, he just adds or subtracts the centimeters necessary so that the outcome can be positive. When we are experiencing a drought, like poor Herman was, God steps in and gives us the opportunity to go on a successful run. Often it can be hard to see the centimeters that make a difference—perhaps the hope he has added to a troubled addict—but we can certainly see the successful run that follows. God supplies exactly what we need to come out winners.

The only problem that remains—the reason we still have losses—is that we forget that God is maintaining our high-level needs. Like Jenna in her search for water, we start to forage for ourselves instead of trusting in our heavenly president. We try to manipulate our own defining moments. The result of our effort is typically tragedy. Society often tells us to be the "master of our own destinies," but this means we are demoting God from his rightful presidential role. Our defining moments will not be positive if we seize control of them.

When I look over my years on this planet, I see thousands of personal experiences. Perhaps only ten or twenty of these experiences actually changed the entire course of my life, some positively, some negatively. These are my defining moments. More specifically, these are the moments that define who I am today. When I controlled these moments, my life was a mess. When I submitted to God as president of my life, these moments directed me toward success. Whenever we let God work in our defining moments, individually or collectively, the future will become continually brighter.

Defining moments have incredible power. The defining moments in my life have brought me from a drug-induced, go-nowhere state to a place of hope and faith. God knows just what we need, and he's watching over us. And for many of us, and society as a whole, he is waiting for those defining moments so he can jump in and make a difference. All we have to do is keep trusting in God, trusting that he knows what we need and, like any good president or leader, he will provide it.

> And this same God who takes care of me will supply all your needs from his glorious riches.
>
> Philippians 4:19a (NLT)

Swat Team

God is in the defining moments of life. From a strategic perspective, it makes sense; these moments are the subtle evidence that God is active yet often undetectable. At the same time, when I look at those defining moments, many of them don't seem very God ordained at all. In fact, most of them felt downright awful as I went through them.

In my personal life, especially when my search for God was in the early phases, every defining moment I had seemed bad. Things just were not going my way—we all know what that feels like. I wished God would just show up and tell me what I was supposed to do. Why did I have to go through that rollover accident? Why did I have to get busted with pot? Why did my girlfriend have to go to the hospital? It just didn't make sense to me that God was behind these potentially defining moments. I thought he was on the side of good, but all these things seemed bad. All I got for wanting God's help was a bunch of hassles in my life.

Jenna can be a hassle too. She's not an overly naughty dog, but she has her lapses. Left on her own for long periods of time, she can certainly find something naughty to do. She has a tendency to follow her nose into trouble. For this reason my wife and I have gone to great lengths to dog proof the apartment, keeping all food items up in cupboards and well out of Jenna's reach. Most of the time it works pretty well. Sometimes it doesn't.

One day I came home as usual and opened the apartment door. It was the typical energetic Jenna greeting, but when I wandered into the kitchen, it appeared that it had not been a typical Jenna day. Apparently Jenna's super-sensitive nose had detected some tiny store of tantalizing crumbs somewhere within the pile of pots and pans sitting on the stove. Unable to resist the urge, she had taken advantage of her size and pulled the stack of pans onto the floor so she could get at them. The kitchen floor was a mess of dirty stoveware.

Though I was upset with Jenna, I was also a little amused with the trouble she got into. I could imagine her sniffing around the kitchen, trying to find the source of that scent that was begging her attention. I pictured her up on her hind legs, front paws on the stove, pulling gingerly on the pans with her teeth until the whole mass crashed to the floor. She must have freaked out when they hit. I bet it was a humorous sight.

Still, I had a bit of a problem. Jenna had been a bad dog, and something needed to be done. The main issue we had was that I spoke English, and she really didn't understand squat. I would be wasting my breath to try to explain to Jenna why this behavior was unacceptable. We found ourselves in the middle of a major communication breakdown.

Fortunately I knew Jenna's psychology pretty much inside out. And I knew a way to get through to her despite the fact that she couldn't understand my words. I knew that if nothing else in the world would motivate her to improve her behavior, this "language" would. Even though I was amused by her mischief, even though I truly cared about her, I pulled back my hand and gave her a nice, hard swat on top of her head. This message came in loud and clear.

The most basic language Jenna can understand is pain. Pain was the key in her upbringing to teach her what things were especially unacceptable. The swat tells Jenna I am very displeased with her actions. And the swats keep coming, sometimes harder and harder, if she refuses to change. Eventually, if she accepts the lessons, Jenna can finally understand what actions are wrong. In fact, she can learn to avoid the swat altogether. But if it wasn't for that painful swat, Jenna would ransack the kitchen every day and then defecate in the living room. In the hands of the right disciplinarian, pain can be very effective.

God, being the president, gets to set the rules. We, being selfish humans, often have a hard time figuring those rules out and obeying them. We know there are certain things to avoid, perhaps blatant violations like murder, but there is a lot of gray area under the realm of "obedient." We don't always know what God wants from us, or what he likes or dislikes. Often we fall back on our own definition of a good person, with no real clue what God desires. Our self-reliance can cause us to become very comfortable with what we are doing, be it right or wrong.

So if we are doing something wrong consistently and comfortably, what can we expect? Discipline is the obvious answer. If we're doing wrong, God has to get the message through to us somehow. Maybe our conscience tugs at us. Maybe our friends or family offer us advice. Maybe God even whispers something in our ear. But if we are not listening, if we are not actively trying to figure out what is right by his standards, then perhaps we need a defining moment inserted into our lives. Super-happy defining moments, though they are possible, often do not have the impact of painful experiences. We aren't going to learn anything if all our behavior is positively reinforced. If there is no other way to get through to us, God will pull out all the stops and allow a painful experience into our lives.

Life is a high-stakes game, and the stakes keep getting higher. If a child hits another child, it's usually a timeout or a scolding. If a teenager hits another teenager, we might be talking about suspension or expulsion. If an adult hits another adult, it's assault and battery, and possibly prison time. It would be great if we could stay kids forever, but we can't. Jenna isn't allowed to make puppy mistakes now that she is older. As we mature, the pain of life keeps getting more and more intense until we discover the solution.

We've talked about God's wisdom—he knows the solution. We've talked about his power—he knows *how to* execute the solution. And we've talked about his method—defining moments, some painful. We need to understand that pain is often not just for pain's sake, but instead it is a strong indicator that we need some sort of adjustment. We don't always know what is wrong, and we don't always understand God's purposes. But we can listen and learn, or we can live in pain forever.

Don't get me wrong here; pain is not always a direct message from God or an indication that a person is living life wrong. Pain is inevitable for the ultra-religious and atheist alike. But when we're looking for God, we can't misinterpret pain. God is smart enough to know how to use it to our advantage, so we learn to live better. When we look at the pain in our lives, we need to look at the circumstance as well, to see if perhaps there is something we need to change. The measure of a man is not necessarily how much pain he can cope with but instead how much he can learn from the pain he experiences. Remember, wisdom is right in front of us, and pain is an excellent opportunity to learn.

I used to wonder all the time why my life was going so miserably. "What have I done to deserve all this pain?" I used to ask God. But I wasn't listening to his answer. I was just doing my own thing, trying to cope with my pain. It should have come as no surprise to me (though it did) that he would continue to discipline me in a way that I understood: continued pain. It wasn't so much physical pain, though I understand that quite well too. But my traumatic car accident caused mental pain. My first drug bust and its repercussions contributed stress and financial pain. My girlfriend's ambulance trip, and the ensuing breakup, created and deepened emotional pain. I felt like I was getting swatted over and over.

But suddenly, after a second police bust (or perhaps during it), I had an epiphany—sort of a culmination of all the swats into one revelation moment. If I changed my behavior, got my hand off the forties, and threw out the joints, maybe this painful existence would get better. I basically said, "Okay, God, I get it." I had been trying to quit those habits for a while up to that point with minimal success. But when I understood that my life was going to continue on a downward spiral until I changed my ways, I finally got serious about it. I finally got God's message loud, clear, and impacting. I had a defining moment. And although I knew it wouldn't be easy, I at least figured out the direction I had to take.

Jenna now understands that getting on the counter or pooping in the apartment are huge no nos. It took some smacking to get it through to her. I now genuinely realize that the success I want in life does not coexist with alcohol and drug abuse. God wanted those things out of my life, so he had to hit me where it hurt. I resisted, but I eventually shaped up. And life is better as a result. I am finally smart enough to listen to God's chastening—his painful spankings for a disobedient child. I don't enjoy pain, but I appreciate that he cares enough to correct me.

> For whom the Lord loves he reproves, even as a father corrects the son in whom he delights.
>
> Proverbs 3:12 (NASB)

Stuck Together

Before we were married, Danielle and I spent a lot of time together in various courtship activities. So I indirectly spent a lot of time with Jenna as well. I began to remember my childhood pup Molly and the many joys of dog ownership. But Jenna also helped me to remember some of the annoyances. The first annoyance was that Danielle could not be away from her apartment for much more than eight hours, or Jenna would leave one of her patented surprises on the floor. The second annoyance was that Jenna always got in the way or begged for attention when Danielle and I were trying to watch a movie. The third annoyance was the hair-and-drool combo. But still, Jenna was more fun than she was trouble.

Jenna was also left in a little bit of a dilemma regarding my increasing time with Danielle. It used to be just Jenna and Mommy, but now this new guy was crowding into her mother-pupper bonding time. Not only that, but this guy was beginning to assume a position of authority over this canine. Sometimes he smacked her if she was naughty. Sometimes he told her no. Sometimes he got control of her leash. After the wedding, he even permanently took over her spot on the bed.

Jenna didn't have a choice regarding my presence. I was in the picture for good. She wasn't even invited to the wedding (though Mommy considered it). So Jenna didn't have a chance to bark out an argument when the audience was asked for objections. It didn't matter if I was an annoyance to her. There was absolutely nothing she could do. Jenna was stuck with me in her life.

We are Stuck

We can have a great many philosophies and thoughts and emotions related to God. We can theorize all we want. But when it comes down to this coexistence, we are stuck with him. Humans don't have another planet or universe to which we can run where he won't be able to see us. We have to coexist with him, whether we embrace it or deny it.

It may sound confining, this forced coexistence, but Jenna doesn't look at living with me that way. She knows I give her all sorts of good things—her life is better because of my involvement. Sure, I impose restrictions, but I also allow for incredible benefits. Being connected to a truly caring superior is worth the price of that connection…but it always has a price: submission.

But is God really *caring*? When we look at all the painful things that happen in life, we have a tendency think that God is either a cruel taskmaster or that he's not very involved with humanity. Either scenario paints a picture of a God who is "kind of caring" or "not very caring" or "totally indifferent." Sure, we can agree with his wisdom and power and justice and the logical authority they imply. But what do we truly know about God's intentions? How do we know he is pulling for us?

Can God Care?

We can find evidence for God's benevolence in many places, but the most basic source is the benevolence we find in ourselves. Remember the hope that I found deep inside me—the same hope you have in you? Well, that isn't the only good thing we find on the inside. For some reason, I have a concern for fellow members of the human race. Heck, I have care for things outside of the human race, like silly Jenna. Sometimes my care for others costs my time, money, and other valued resources, yet I still continue to care. By no means is my care limitless, but it is undeniably inside of me and each one of us.

Compared to God, my intelligence is very limited, as are my other traits. If I posses the ability to think, then comparatively God possesses the ability to super duper think. So if I possess the ability to care, what does that mean God has in the care department? If my knowledge is just a tiny fraction of the knowledge God has, then it makes sense that my ability to care is just a tiny fraction of the amount that God can care. Just like any of our other positive traits, God beats us out significantly in the ability to care.

Does God Care?

So he can care for us, but how do we know he does? Well, mainly because of his choice to coexist with us. Poor Jenna is stuck with me; she has no choice. But the same is not true of me. I can leave anytime. If I get fed up with Jenna, I can go take a walk without her. I can shut her in the spare bedroom of the apartment if I want. If I got really fed up with her, I could begin talks with my wife to get Jenna permanently sent away (that would be a can of worms…). I do not have to deal with Jenna any more than I want to. I possess all the power when it comes to our connection.

God is all powerful, which means he can leave this coexistence with humanity anytime he wants. If he got fed up with us, he could be gone tomorrow, just like I can separate myself from Jenna at my discretion. Certainly our naughty human behavior may justify God's leaving us, yet here he is, watching over planet earth. Here he is, doing those little things that help reassure us that he's there. He could choose to be anywhere in the universe or beyond, but he has chosen to interact with humanity. The logical conclusion is that he must care about us.

When legislators develop laws, there seems to be a constant struggle between ideals and reality. I'm sure I would face similar challenges if I were in their shoes. Speaking as an idealist, I would want to develop laws that required a society to be perfect in every way. Speaking as a realist, such laws would either be unenforceable or would eventually lock up every single imperfect human. Idealism and realism have a hard time coexisting within a society that constantly seeks perfection yet cannot help but notice its limitations.

Fortunately, God is different from our society. Not only is he free from the limitations that we have, he has actually achieved the perfection we seek. In God's being, the ideal and the real are exactly the same thing. When God makes decisions about what is right and wrong, he doesn't need to rely on a manual; he *is* the manual. His standards are derived from his nature. The positive feeling God has toward mankind is therefore the "rightest" feeling one being can have for another. God *cared* for humanity long before the word was ever developed or defined.

Yet in God's care for the human race, he doesn't just toss knowledge out the window. He has a practical reason for his decision, and it is much like the reason that I have decided to care for Jenna. It isn't her ability to entertain, or else she would be of no more value to me than a television that poops. It isn't her ability to clean the floors; she is kind of like a vacuum that only works on tasty food morsels. Her value, the reason I care for her more than inanimate objects, is that she has the potential for a *two-sided* connection. Care given to a television set is wasted. Care given to Jenna is something I can receive back from her. She has the capacity to care about me.

God cares about humankind. He cares because he can. He cares because it's the right thing to do—part of his nature. And he cares because we possess the ability to care back. Jenna may never know how much I care, though I prove my affection with the time and money and petting I invest in her. But she can show just a shred of appreciation for the things I do for her. When I come home, she can greet me excitedly, wagging her tail furiously in anticipation of the good things I can drop into her life. And this shred of appreciation is one of the key building blocks for our connection. This appreciation makes me want to care for her all the more.

God cares about us and deserves our care and appreciation in return. He sees potential in us that we often cannot see ourselves—potential for a two-sided connection with the God of the universe. People embrace this opportunity, people deny it, and people remain indifferent or undecided. If I could choose which of these reactions I want Jenna to have regarding me, it would be the embrace. I would want her to choose to grow closer to me, to learn to appreciate me more. In this way, our connection could grow stronger and stronger. This is exactly what God wants from us.

> "For I know the plans I have for you," says the Lord. "They are plans for good and not for disaster, to give you a future and a hope."
>
> Jeremiah 29:11 (NLT)

Bed Bugged

Humankind understands the value of connection, at least to some degree. We have many important relationships with each other. Obviously, connection is something God values as well, prompting his involvement with the earth. But at the same time, there seems to be boatloads of hindrances that hurt human ability to connect, both with each other and with God.

God is a God of extremes. He is *the* high end of the intelligence scale, the power scale, the justice scale, and especially the goodness scale. He is *perfectly* good, good to the extreme. Humans, on the other hand, are not always so good. That is one of the prime reasons we have a hard time connecting with God. We spend a lot of time in the kinda-good-but-with-a-little-evil zone. Sometimes we know what's right and wrong but choose wrong. Most of the time when we mess up, we aren't sure what's what, and so we accidentally choose wrong. Regardless, we are known for many of our bad decisions and the problems that result.

We live in a fallen world, a world riddled with evils. Who God is and what he is doing are often obscured by various circumstances and distractions. It is easy to forget about God when we are under the gun. And when we forget about God, we default our allegiance to the "smartest person" we know—ourselves.

Despite Jenna being stuck with me, she really has wonderful freedoms. She never has to worry about food or water. She gets plenty of outdoor time and exercise. She has the run of the apartment. She is showered with treats. All of this provision is at her disposal as long as she generally remembers that I am the "president" of the apartment. But Jenna doesn't always remember.

Before I came onto the scene, Mommy had let Jenna sleep on the bed with her. Once I was in the picture, things changed a little. In the early going, Jenna was banned entirely from the bed, which she took in stride. After a little coaxing from Mommy, I finally caved in and let Jenna lie on the bed while we would read at night. But after I was finished reading, I wanted Jenna to lie on the floor. The problem was that Jenna was pretty comfortable with her position on the bed. When asked, she would usually move very begrudgingly from her position.

One night in particular I told her, "Jenna, get down," and motioned to the floor. She didn't move—just kind of acting asleep. I intensified my tone and repeated myself. She still didn't even acknowledge me, though I knew she heard me. "Down!" I said again. This time she gave me kind of a low growl, indicative of her defiance. I was not pleased with that gesture, and I grabbed her collar and pulled her off the bed. Continuing her insubordination, she growled louder and even nipped at me. At this, I smacked her hard and made her go to her pout spot. This was one of the harshest confrontations I had ever had with the pup. Finally she realized that she was wrong and submitted.

I know Jenna is a kind and affectionate dog through and through. I know she didn't mean to oppose me and was very sorry afterward. But the fact of the matter is that our little altercation hurt my connection with her, albeit temporarily. I thought that she and I were close, but apparently a spot on the bed was more important to her than my authority. Her choice greatly disappointed me.

So my wife and I had to make a decision about what to do about Jenna's little rebellion. I could not coexist with Jenna in an environment that she did not give me the authority. Jenna had already shown that she was willing to give me the appropriate respect elsewhere throughout the apartment. It was just in the bed department that she apparently struggled. So the simple solution to keeping our connection strong was to eliminate this opportunity for her to defy me. To put it simply, Jenna is no longer allowed on the bed when we are reading at night.

Poor Jenna often wonders why she can't hop up on the bed. She comes over to my side and then over to Mommy's, looking at us longingly. I feel bad that she isn't disciplined enough to obey everywhere. Those puppy-dog eyes are never easy to resist. But I know for the sake of my connection with her, I have to enforce this rule. I have to keep her in a place in which she will behave so that our connection will not weaken.

Strengthening Connections

God is all about keeping and strengthening his connection with us. Contrarily, the world we live in is filled with things that can potentially hurt this connection. And although we cannot perceive many of these connection breakers, God can. In fact, it is along those lines that God draws up many of his regulations for us. If an activity will strengthen our connection with him, he invites it. If an activity will hurt our connection, he discourages it, sometimes with a healthy but painful swat.

Life in general, with or without the pursuit of God, can be very mundane. When we begin to make more of an effort to seek after God, sometimes we expect things to turn awesome overnight. We look at God with our puppy-dog eyes and ask for a million bucks or an Escalade or an attractive girlfriend or boyfriend. But there are many times when we don't get what we want. This is not evidence of God's unkindness but simply our inability to handle what we are asking for. God knows that many of these requests will get in the way of our relationship with him. It doesn't mean we can never have them; it means we aren't ready for them yet. With a million bucks, for example, we might forget about God and do our own thing, so it is logical for God to *not* grant that request.

The more we mess up, the more it becomes obvious that we are doing the wrong thing. It doesn't mean it is easy to break bad habits; it just means we have no excuse not to. When I was heavy in the party scene, I could see the direction it was taking me. Aside from the defining moments, I also had daily indicators related to health, finances, and overall emotional state—indicators that told me I was going the wrong way. Why was this way wrong for me? Because it continuously hurt my connection with God (weak as it was). So I had to begin to make an effort to stay away from the crowds and locations that contributed to my delinquency. It is obvious that a person struggling with alcohol should not go to the bar any more than a dog struggling with insubordination should be on the bed.

God began to eliminate connection breakers in my life, and I began to help him. My probation and urine testing—results of a defining-moment police bust—went a long way in helping me keep my system clean of drugs. And my fear that I could not control my pot-smoking tendencies forced me to remain reasonably sober when hanging with my friends. The connection I was developing with God was becoming two sided; I was trying to do my part too. Granted, he still seemed miles away, like a distant president, but he was there nonetheless. I soon began to realize that he was all about connection. He wanted to be involved in my life.

Well, here we run into a dilemma because it isn't just God and me on the planet. There are billions of people here. God's role as president is anything but easy, especially from our limited perspective. He can't please all the people all the time, and many of his decisions are quite unpopular with the general public. When God makes a decision, there are two sides to be on: benefited or not benefited.

Either the decision helps us or it hurts us. So the question is, how do we make sure we are on the benefited side of the decisions God makes? Do we have to be some clean-cut, in-church-every-Sunday, read-through-the-Bible-in-a-year-type people? What does it take to receive the benefits of God?

To answer that question, I again look to my silly puppy Jenna and her Mommy, Danielle. My wife's love of animals affects every aspect of my life. Of course, Jenna is the first indication of my wife's affection for animals. Then there are the two birds and the two fish that she had when we got married. Then there are the frequent requests for a second dog, or a new bird, or whatever her cute little heart is set on that particular day. I appreciate this childlike quality in my wife.

I can't get away from Danielle's love of animals even when we're watching TV. If my wife has the remote, there is a good chance the channel will "get stuck" on *America's Funniest Animals*, or some other show like that. Sometimes it is one of those show-dog shows, like the Westminster. All those prissy dogs prancing around next to their strict owners, it seems kind of silly to me. And then I look over and see Jenna chewing on a cardboard box. The show seems even sillier.

Which dog is the right dog for me? Which dog will have the benefit of my kindness? Is it "Prancer" or is it "Box-chewer"? Well, for me it's Box-chewer. The reason I choose box-chewing Jenna over any of those other highly trained dogs is simple: we have a connection. This relationship cancels out skill or ability or looks or background. I care for Jenna just as she is, shortcomings and all. Not only that, but she has decided to accept me as well. Mutual acceptance results in our connection—a connection I hope to continue building.

So who is God going to benefit with his decisions? It isn't the skillful or the well-educated or the ultra-religious (necessarily). It is the people with whom he has a connection. It is the people who understand that this is a two-sided link that we have with our heavenly president and make an effort to build their side. It is the people who try to keep those connection-breakers out of their lives. It isn't easy keeping this connection strong, but the best things in life are never easy. And God is sure to honor our efforts.

We can see that God is all about developing connections. And "developing" means that this connection is always moving forward, getting better, growing deeper. He may have the qualifications and authority to be the president, and this may be his initial goal. But he wants more than that. He wants to see us blossom and flourish. He wants to see us succeed. And so that we can fulfill these goals, he wants more than anything that we develop our connection to him so he can help us. God has all the good things we truly want out of life, and he's asking us to come to him and get them.

> Draw close to God, and God will draw close to you. Wash your hands, you sinners; purify your hearts, you hypocrites.
>
> James 4:8 (NLT)

Part 3:

God and Community:
The Purpose of the Church

God the Boss

Knowing who the president of the United States is and the attributes of his office are necessary precursors to developing any kind of connection to him. But at the same time, knowing about him and who he is, and even living in his country, really doesn't provide any sort of guarantee for a person. Don't get me wrong; America is great, and loaded with rights. Among these rights, however, is the right to be poor and the right to be hungry and the right to be miserable and the right to be depressed. Just acknowledging and even revering the president does not free you from the dangers of life and especially the emotional burdens. You can know all about the president and still be miserable.

Many people have the God trivia down pat, but their lives are still in shambles. The reason is there is no real benefit in simply knowing *about* God and skipping the connection. Knowing about God is definitely important for establishing and growing a connection with him. But it doesn't do any good to understand God *can* help you if you don't reach out and take the help he gives. Here again action is key—transforming what you *know* into what you *practice.*

The president of the United States is a busy man, so he does not have the time to get to know every American personally. God, however, is not limited in this way. In all likelihood, the average US resident will never have a solid connection with the president, but we do have every opportunity to get to know God better. And unlike any earthly connection with a person or country, a connection with God *does* guarantee certain things. In one way or another, God will always be there for us. He takes care of his team better than any earthly ruler can.

Many times people are content to put God into a presidential role in their lives, but they stop there. There are a number of reasons for ceased development, and people usually try to justify themselves quickly on the basis of effort. "Well, I've given 2 percent of my time to God, so that should suffice." And while it is not my right to judge if anyone's effort is sufficient, I will say that if I find a stock that guarantees to pay out large dividends, I would be a fool not to invest as much as I could possibly afford. Lack of investment is a lack of belief that God's system will pay off. If we only invest minimal resources, we have to expect minimal return.

It can be a challenge to invest more of ourselves in God. The number-one reason people do not go further with him is that it's not easy. Sometimes pursuit of God is misconstrued as "the easy life" in an attempt to get more people into church. But if there is one thing I've come to understand through my search, it is that trying to live for God is the hardest challenge we can undertake. It is an all-out war against our human nature and our desire to consume 100 percent of our time on ourselves. It isn't easy for anybody. But why is it so tough? The same reason military boot camp is so tough—God is looking for maximum development. Without a challenge, we don't become stronger.

I became comfortable with the idea of God being a presidential figure, but I didn't feel like my connection to him was all that strong. I recognized that his part was to make the major choices about right and wrong, and my responsibility was to acknowledge and accept them. I felt like I was kind of a citizen in God's general community, but not much more. I *wanted* to be more though, again with the reasoning that drawing closer to God must be a rewarding experience. So I made my general token efforts to build my connection with him: a little exploratory Bible reading, a little casual prayer, and a little church attendance.

Church was an interesting place. I had been in many churches growing up but had promptly ceased attending when I became independent of my parents. When I finally decided to return on my own to the church scene years later, some things had changed, and some things were the same. The music at the church I began attending was more modern and contemporary than I had known, and I enjoyed the atmosphere. The preaching wasn't as dry as I had remembered; it was a little more upbeat and interactive (or I was more responsive). But the message I heard from the songs and the sermons was something I recognized from my younger days: "Don't do this, don't do that..."

Society has some general regulations that are undoubtedly God ordained; I understood this. Rules like some of the ones we find in the Ten Commandments have become foundational for our society. Our legal system acknowledges rules like "Thou shalt not kill" and "Thou shalt not steal," and most citizens of God's community abide by these laws. Other commandments like "Thou shalt not bear false witness" and "Thou shalt not commit adultery" have become more of a social guideline system, subject to circumstance. Rules like "Thou shalt not covet" and "Honor thy father and thy mother" have all but gone out the window for society in general. Many professing believers, God's "citizens," no longer abide by most of the traditional regulations. Instead, they have a tendency to pick and choose whatever suits them best.

But the church is different from general society. Many churches have those same commandments posted all over the place—and all ten of them! And as the message of a church develops, it becomes apparent that there are about a thousand more commandments besides. Where society stops at a general adoption of several of God's rules, the church affirms the continuing importance of most, if not all, of these regulations. And while no church or churchgoer is perfect, they are going beyond just the "citizenship" of general society—an ambiguous belief in God. Many of these church people have actually become what seem to be God's "workers." They may have normal jobs, but they have made God's regulations a part of their everyday lives. They are trying to do what God wants wherever they go, not just in the church building.

Working for God

Living in America under the president of the United States does not make life perfect. But it does open a world of opportunities to the citizen, opportunities not available in every country. You aren't guaranteed a job, but you are given the opportunity to work. If you take this opportunity to work and make the most of it, your life can improve. Our entire social and economic structure is based on work and its results. If we all did exactly what we wanted when we wanted, we would have a chaotic, authorityless society that would not advance. So much hard work has gone into the development of America to date, and probably a lack of hard work is what often ails us today. Anything of lasting value requires some amount of work.

Sure, when you enter the work world you are forced into a new, tighter set of regulations than the listless citizen. In a free country, a person can sleep until noon every day if he wants. But if you get a job—become an employee—there's a good chance that you will have to get up at seven in the morning or earlier. If you don't get up on time, you may be *exiting* the work world as quickly as you entered. So why on earth would you confine yourself with this and other regulations? Because you like the benefits that a job provides you. Money, stability, and structure are all good reasons to work.

So what do we expect from God? Do we expect to collect unemployment forever? A God who cares, who is concerned about our development, would never allow idleness to prevail. A life with God is filled with benefits, but sometimes we have to put in some work to secure them. We can't just live how we want and expect God to smile cheerfully upon us forever. It is for our own good, as well as society's in general, that we seize the opportunity to work.

Three major misconceptions characterize society's view of working for God. The first misconception is that we don't have to work. Some people see God as an entertainer or a Sunday-morning event and not much more. Granted, many of the things he gives us are entirely unearned, much like the food and water I give to Jenna. She doesn't have to pay a price to exist, necessarily, and God likewise gives us many unearned things just because he cares. He sees something in us worth cultivating; we can be more than just useless pet sea monkeys. But we have to *do* more than sea monkeys if we want to build a connection. And sometimes *work* is something we have to do. Nobody's life is a continual frolic through the roses. Not working, especially on our personal development, is an indication that we do not think we need work or that we think we are hopeless. Either is an entirely self-centered viewpoint. Compared to God, all of us need work, but at the same time no one is hopeless.

The second major misconception, the one that I had, is that the *only* thing God's "employees" do is work. They seem to work to abide by every tiny rule, and then after that they work to find even more rules. Eventually these rules seem to crowd out fun and relaxation and having a life in general. Sometimes the avidly religious can appear this way. But most of those people aren't working for the sake of work or because they love rules and regulations. They are working, *and* they are being benefited, sometimes in obvious ways and sometimes in not-so-obvious ways. Certainly God is aware of our human limitations and is trustworthy enough to provide rest and fun in our lives. He is also aware of the dangers of excessive relaxation when it becomes a lazy lifestyle. As with anything, balance is important here, and God, as boss, must be left in charge of what the appropriate balance is.

The third misconception is probably the most dangerous. Some people, churchgoers and general public alike, think that working for

God can be part-time. They put in their shift on Sunday morning and relax for another week once the service is over. They do whatever they want for six-and-a-half days and then try to behave for a couple hours at church. We obviously have the right to do this in America and as God's "citizens." But it really shouldn't surprise us when our part-time effort yields *part-time benefits*. We can't expect to obey God for a few minutes and have a solid connection.

My wife and I have a lot of regulations for Jenna's coexistence with us. One of those regulations is that she obviously can't eat off our plates, unless, of course, we give the food to her. One morning my wife was in a rush, doing a million things at once, and she set her breakfast plate on the bed for a minute and went down the hall to do something else. Jenna normally follows my wife around incessantly, but for some reason, Jenna did not follow her down the hall. My wife remembered the eggs and turned around quickly.

Jenna was sitting there, sniffing in the air. She was on the trail of something. Seconds later, she noticed the eggs sitting on the bed, well within her reach. She looked down the hall at Danielle, then back at the eggs. "Don't you dare…" my wife threatened. Jenna looked back at Danielle, then the aroma of the scrumptious breakfast caught her nose again, and she looked back at the eggs. My wife quickly did what she had gone down the hall to do; it only took seconds. When she turned and looked, the eggs had mysteriously vanished off the plate. Whether Jenna was a magician or just a greedy doggy didn't matter; she was in big trouble.

Jenna is not allowed to take breaks from her obedience. Coexisting with me and my wife, Jenna, must obey our rules *all* the time. If she were to choose a day of the week that she would be pooping wherever she got the urge, then she would also be indirectly choosing a day of the week that her punishment was heavy and her life was miserable. If she chose only one day that she was obedient, then it would be questionable whether we could even allow her in our apartment. Jenna has to see me as her boss every day of every week, or swats, scolds, and timeouts would be a constant part of her life. She cannot be a part-time puppy.

Let me pause here to say that there is nothing necessarily wrong with going to church experimentally, like I did. It is a step in the process to develop the discipline to attend church or to change a disobedient lifestyle. The key word, however, is *step*. I started by giving God only a small part of my time. As I began to understand more about him, I realized that not only did he want more of my life; he wanted more of my life *so he could make it better*. Every time I resisted, it was an obvious sign that I did not truly believe God would improve my life. It was a direct disagreement with who God is. As we begin to see the importance of a connection with God, we need to take steps forward, like moving him from president to boss in our lives. If we are only going to church on Christmas and Easter, there is a pretty solid indication that we do not trust in God much at all.

Herein is the danger of the part-time believer. If we say we believe in God but are the exact same people we were when we didn't believe in God, then perhaps we don't truly believe. If we did believe in God, how could we not get on his self-improvement plan—his "steps to success"? Granted, it is a process, but it is also an ongoing test of our connection and commitment to the one who is above us. When we only obey God part time, we are failing that test. And much like success has sort of a sweet-smelling aroma to it, failure has a stink. When people smell this stink exuding from professing believers, those people do not want what these "believers" have. This is why so many people are repulsed by Christians or church—because there are many hypocrites out there. People who say they believe but do not believe enough to acknowledge, accept, and abide by God's regulations on a day-to-day basis are not really believers at all. They are tourists who like to see the sights but not pay the price. Certainly we all slip up, but if we do not commit to a connection with God, we will always return home to the same mess in our lives.

God is in the business of taking people to the next level. It is a cooperative effort, like any business partnership. If we do not put our hands to the plow, we will never harvest the crop. But if we are willing to work for God's purpose, we will see benefits beyond our wildest dreams.

> For the Scripture says, "Do not keep an ox from eating as it treads out the grain." And in another place, "Those who work deserve their pay!"
>
> 1 Timothy 5:18 (NLT)

Mr. and Mrs. Pack Man

I've heard it said on many occasions, "I don't need to go to church to have a connection with God." In fact, I've probably said it many times before and even convinced myself that it was true. Of course, my motivation was that I was too lazy to go to church and not that my connection to God was so impressive. And while God is not necessarily tallying church attendance to see who his favorites are, I suspect most of the time people avoid church for selfish reasons rather than religious ones. Regardless of motivation, the question becomes, *how important is church to our connection with God?*

I think Jenna and I have a good connection. Most of the time, she appropriately views me as her boss—the guy in charge. Aside from the occasional slip up, Jenna is usually pretty well behaved when she is in our apartment. But life cannot be lived entirely inside the safety and warmth of a home. She likes to go out to play, and she loves to make new doggy friends. In our apartment complex, Jenna has already made many friends. There's Oscar the wiener dog who excitedly submits to Jenna's towering size. There's Dottie the pouty bulldog who walks under Jenna's body like it is her own personal garage. There's Buster the golden doodle puppy who is too young to realize Jenna could smoosh him. And Jenna has friends outside the complex as well. She loves to go to Maggie's house and run laps with the golden-retriever-yellow-Lab mix. A different Maggie, another energetic golden doodle, loves to annoy Jenna into chasing her. Jenna has a "twin" named Angel the yellow Lab. They like to just chill out together. Jenna has countless other doggy buddies at my friends' and family's houses. She's a very sociable dog.

Whenever Jenna sees another dog in our apartment complex, all bets are off. She drops her toy or stops her sniffing and makes a beeline for the new potential friend. Most of the time Jenna is on a leash, so she just yanks with all her might, hoping I will take her over to greet the new buddy. And I usually give in because I know how much she likes to meet other dogs. I know it is in her nature to be part of a doggy community.

It's hard to visualize Jenna in the wild, but as I understand it, she would be part of a pack of dogs. She certainly is no lone wolf. Dogs have a tendency to "pack up" and work in teams to find prey or do whatever else they do (again, hard to see Jenna as a hunter of anything more than marshmallows). Jenna and her posse would prowl the woods, looking for rabbits or squirrels or skunks to eat, searching for comfortable bedding, or just chasing each others' tails. This communal behavior is natural for dogs, and it aids in their survival. Two dogs have a lot better chance of cornering a darting bunny than does one. And I think having another dog there to help is enjoyable no matter what the circumstance. It's good to have a friend with a common purpose.

I am well aware of Jenna's natural inclination to run with a pack. In fact, I support her socializing completely—to a degree. Jenna is happier and healthier if she has these doggy friends. But at the same time, I do not let her run off and do whatever she wants with her friends. If she did, she may inadvertently put herself in danger or forgetfully sever the connection she has with me. I want her to have the benefit of these friendships, but I do not want her to experience the dangers of abandoning me. As long as my connection with Jenna remains strong, she can play with her buddies as much as she wants. I want her to be happy.

Human beings, like dogs, have social tendencies. We like to run with a pack. If that pack runs into success, we're there. If that pack runs into failure, we're usually there too. Regardless, it feels good to be part of a team. It feels good to have common goals and to share successes and failures. Most of all, it feels good to belong.

God is not ignorant of this human tendency; in fact, he supports it. He wants us to find friends that we can run with. But like my wishes for Jenna, he wants us to have friends that will not get us into trouble. God does not want us or our friends to jeopardize our safety or our connection with him. He knows that the right pack can be very beneficial, but the wrong pack can be doom. And his response to this knowledge is simple: he provides a pack that is running in the right direction. He provides the church.

Support

In my partying days, I became a member of a group known as the Drink and Smoke 'til You Can't No More gang. Okay, we really didn't have a formal title, but that's what we did nearly every night. We supported each other in all the drinking and smoking, encouraging reckless behaviors of many varieties. As a result, we all helped each other to adopt some severe addictions. We dug a hole together, and much of the time we each struggled to get out of it alone. I eventually became exactly like the pack I had chosen.

I had lots of support in doing the wrong things, as most of us do. I soon realized that if I was to do the right things, I was going to need some support in that effort as well. This is one of the strengths of the organization God has assembled. The church provides us the support we need to stay on the right path. As I began to attend church, I found people who had achieved the same types of successes that I hoped to achieve. So I started to hang around. And as that group of people worked to help me out, I began to see the power of good support. I started to adopt the positive traits of this new pack, and I continue to work to develop those traits today.

Education

I love the social support that the church provides for me. But that isn't all I get out of the church community. As I mentioned, when my search for God began, I felt grossly unqualified and ignorant. While my need for community was deep-seated, my theology was superficial (though I tried to hide this fact). Church—the right church—provides a place where a person can increase his religious IQ and better understand what exactly this God fellow is all about. There are so many people who do not know or have a correct understanding of what Christianity entails. Church can be very beneficial in providing proper guidance.

Foundation

I find both the social support and the practical teaching of the church are very important. But there is a third facet of the church community that has great value to me. When I walk around at work or the mall or a sporting event, I see tons of people. What do I know about these people? Not much. I don't know if they are friendly or mean. I don't know if they like me or hate me. I have no idea what their moral system is like. So my reaction to these people is usually a defensive one. I usually don't say much, and we pass by each other like ships in the night, sometimes with not so much as eye contact. Even if I do say something, trying to be friendly, I quickly back off if the other person does not share my good-naturedness.

However, things change when I am at church. It isn't because I become a different person or anything; I just know something about the other people there. I know we have something in common. I know we have some of the same values and believe in some of the same rules. I know that we are both seeking God, at least to some extent, as evidenced by our attendance. So I am much more likely to give a friendly greeting, and I am much more likely to receive one back.

At a church, people have this general sense of goodwill toward others. For some people it may be an act, but for others it is definitely genuine. Why the sense of goodwill? In part, it is because of those darn rules! The church rules tell us that we should not hate one another. They tell us we should not act mean or judgmentally (that one is violated a lot). Regardless of what people do to us, we should not curse them. The rules tell us to live peaceably with one another. So that means if a person I pass in the church halls flips me off, that person is breaking the rules they believe in. I know that person is either internally conflicted (convicted) because of his rule breakage, or that he doesn't belong at the church at all.

I don't flip people off at church, but I don't always know all the rules either. No one can make the claim that they are perfect. But the church is an organization built on a very high moral system—higher than the American legal system. It is a tough system to abide by, no doubt, but it is an admirable system as well. Its focus is right and wrong *as determined by God,* and not by man. And part of the beauty of the system is that the support is built in. When we treat others with kindness, we are obeying the regulations *and* strengthening our connections to those in our pack. Sounds like an intelligent setup.

Pack Up

We are inevitably going to interact with thousands, if not millions, of people over the course of our lives. Packs are guaranteed to form all around us. Some will form because of locality—because people live close to each other or work together. Some will form based on surface-level likes and dislikes, like a Euchre club or a Detroit Lions fan club. And some packs will form because of commonalities at the deepest level, like the pursuit of God or higher morals. If we believe in God and we believe in the value of community, it is a simple step to combine the two. Finding a loving, accepting, morally-sound church is the best way to assure that we get the support we need to carry on the pursuit of God throughout the week. It is the best way to make sure our Christian work actually works.

The bottom line is that we are fooling ourselves if we think we can live for God without help from anyone. A decision not to go to church is often an indication that we believe we *can* do it alone, or that we're not even interested in trying. The danger of this mindset is obvious. God knows the value of community, and he has factored it into his program. He wants us to have friends we can support and who can support us right back. He wants us to be educated in his precepts. He wants us to build our lives on morals that are above our own—*his* morals. But he doesn't want us to do it alone; he wants us to do it as a team.

> Though one may be overpowered, two can defend themselves. A cord of three strands is not quickly broken.
>
> Ecclesiastes 4:12 (NIV)

A Tight Leash

Church is a great support system for pursuing a connection with God. There is strength in numbers. Yet many people avoid the church—even professing believers. Sometimes it is the churchgoers themselves who are a big turn-off for prospective attendees. But more often than not, it is that long list of religious rules and regulations that cause people to avoid the church scene. Nobody seems to want to give up perceived freedoms, not even for a great reward. People don't want to take the challenge of living under God's program.

We've already talked about God's first communication technique, pain. If we don't seem to have the ability to listen to God's commands, he will inevitably try to direct our lives toward him with some attention-grabbing pain. I know that when my life got miserable, I finally started trying to listen. And I soon realized that although pain is a very effective language, God can speak in other ways too.

I told you about Jenna and the pots, pans, poops, and other naughtiness. Each instance garnered for her at least a swat or two so Jenna could understand the message in terms she knew. But while I was smacking her, I also verbalized my displeasure, despite Jenna's poor English comprehension. I kept it real simple most of the time, sternly telling her no.

For a while, Jenna heard it so much that I'm sure she began to believe *no* was her name. But she eventually got the picture. Although the swats were effective, Jenna soon figured out that if she would listen to my *no* she would be able to avoid some of those painful smacks. If I tell her no before she acts and she listens and stops, her life is better off. It didn't take her long to put this knowledge to good use.

These days, she doesn't get swatted nearly as much because she has learned to listen to the *no*. If I drop a candy bar on the floor, Jenna's first instinct is to go for it. But when I say no, she stops and by doing so avoids further disciplinary actions. She is clueless as to what I am saying most of the time, but *no* she recognizes. When she hears that word, she shapes up.

We certainly have the right to let God communicate with us through pain if we want. We can live our entire lives in rebellion but should not be surprised by the agony that follows. But we do have the option of trying to figure out God's other communication techniques and avoid the pain of rule breaking. If we can hear him tell us no, we can cut down our painful moments significantly. But here again we struggle with hearing God on our own, especially in the early stages of the search for him.

What should we do when we struggle? Well, we should turn to the people who might be able to help us understand what God doesn't want us to do—what his *no*s are. We should consult the more experienced members of our pack, the church. And what seems to be the first word we learn? *No.* The church has many rules that give us guidance on what God may not want us to do. Sure, these rules may seem strict or fun ruining, much like my rules probably seem to Jenna. But if we can learn to abide by these rules, we are going to avoid a lot of future pain. It seems like a worthy trade off to me. Plus I've got the church to support me, so abiding by the rules should be doable.

But why all the rules? Why would God care about what I do here on earth, especially my "less-significant" actions? Why do I have to avoid things like drunkenness and fornication and a bad temper, things that used to be on my fun list?

The first reason to obey the rules is connection, as mentioned before. When we live in a way that God does not agree with, we hurt our connection with the source of good. He can't reward this behavior, and usually it bears punishment. Just like an employer is going to terminate their connection with a lazy, disobedient worker, so God as boss cannot allow his workers to do more harm than good. God wants to maintain a top-quality connection with us.

The second reason to obey is development. Our connection with God cannot go to the next level if our submissiveness does not go to the next level. We begin as citizens of God's nation, but that's not all he wants from us. Since he encourages the move from citizen to worker, it is a sure indication he wants to see advancement in our behavior. Like any caring boss, he wants the best for his workers. He wants to see us promoted. Learning to better understand and abide by his rules is what facilitates our advancement and helps us grow.

The third reason we should obey is probably the most practical. There is danger out there—danger we can't always see.

I have many rules for Jenna—rules she may think are silly—but every single one serves a purpose. Rules against Jenna on the bed keep her from misbehaving and hurting her relationship with me. Rules against pooping in the house not only preserve connection but they advance her to a level that makes her a better dog, a house-broken dog. But violation of these rules does not put her into any direct danger from anyone but me. I might come down on her for her misbehavior, but she will certainly get another thousand chances before I ever do anything to permanently remove her from the safety of the apartment.

But outside of the apartment is a world that is not so forgiving. Outside there are dangers, some of which Jenna cannot comprehend. Most significant of these dangers are the driveways and parking areas inside the apartment complex. Cars buzz through these internal roadways throughout the day. Jenna could easily run out into the path of an oncoming car, entirely oblivious, and that would be the end. Other dangers include some not-so-friendly dogs in the complex, and perhaps even Jenna's own attention deficit disorder, which gives her a tendency to stray.

There is a need for a protective rule here. To meet this need, we have instituted a no-going-outside-without-a-leash rule. It would be great if the entire world was dog friendly, but it isn't. So instead of risking Jenna's well-being, the leash rule forces her to be tethered to a source of safety—me. She is very limited in what she can do with the leash on: she can't act on whims, she can't naughtily chase after things, and she has to constantly keep me in mind. But she will remain safe as long as she stays beside me.

I can see the dangers Jenna doesn't understand. God can see danger we can't see. Sure, God has many rules that may not make a lot of sense to us. But I have to assume that he has a lot better foresight than I do. I might be able to see the physical dangers around me, but God can see the moral and spiritual dangers. And you know, he was right about drunkenness; it got me nothing but trouble. Same with fornication and my temper. We are welcome to see how these dangers play out in our lives, but we are much smarter if we can trust God and avoid the negative results altogether.

I used to run from God, but I realized that there are deadly dangers in life that I cannot navigate on my own. I can't even see them. On the ride of life, I can hope to not run into these dangers, or I can stick close to God and abide by his constraints. I don't like being leashed very much, but I *really* don't like being oblivious to death on my doorstep. The benefits of staying close to God are worth the price that it costs.

Jenna really is a great dog. I've seen many dogs struggle and fight when it was time to put the leash on. But not Jenna. She runs excitedly to where the leash hangs and looks at it longingly. Once I grab it off the wall, she sits in antsy anticipation, waiting for me to put it on her. She might not like the thing all that much, but she knows what it means. She is smart enough to realize that the leash means she gets to go outside. She gets to sniff around and play around and meet new friends, all under the safety of her caring boss. I appreciate her submissive attitude, and I reward her with as much freedom as I can give her while still keeping her safe.

God does the same for us. If we can embrace his rule system, even though it might sometimes hold us back from things that look good to us, then we can stay safe beside our caring boss. We should look at the rule system as a means by which we can be close to God, not as a restraint. True happiness, joy, and even fun can be found abiding by the rules of the wise master. Once we realize God's intentions, obedience becomes the obvious choice.

> He will protect his godly ones, but the wicked will perish in darkness. No one will succeed by strength alone.
>
> 1 Samuel 2:9 (NLT)

Stinky Jenna

Our apartment complex lawn is peppered with land mines. These aren't the type of mines that will blow off a limb; they are more the type that will devastate your sense of smell. Of course, I'm talking about what seems to be developing into one of my apparent favorite topics—dog excrement. While my wife and I are very conscientious about picking up after Jenna, other dog owners can be negligent in this area. On top of that, we have flocks of Canadian geese that like to grace the property with their feces. Suffice it to say that I have to be very careful where I step when I am taking Jenna to the bathroom, or I will find myself scraping out the tread of my tennis shoes with a sharp stick.

Danielle and I have been honing our sense-and-avoid skills for years now, so we can usually circumvent known hazard areas. Jenna, on the other hand, is not so perceptive. If there is a mysterious stench in our apartment, Jenna's paws are the primary suspects. It is not uncharacteristic for her to ignorantly frolic through a pile or two when we are outside. In fact she's even been known to roll around in some of the goose patties. She unknowingly takes that atrocious odor and brings it into our apartment. It isn't long before we all smell it.

I have noticed that even if my wife and I stay super vigilant when we take Jenna out and we make sure that she never even comes within ten feet of any poop, we still run into a similar problem. As time goes by, no matter what we do, Jenna eventually adopts an outdoor odor. She has a distinct dog smell that, if left unattended, will become offensive to the human nose. It is natural for her to smell a bit funky to me.

Stinky Me?

Do you know what smells a bit funky to the nose of God? Humans. Sure, we might be able to admit that the church is a solid social organization and that the rules have some intrinsic value. This is, however, a far cry from the practical step of walking though those church doors. As we see the extensive church regulations unfold before us, two dilemmas become quite apparent. The first is that I personally stink at keeping all those rules. The second is that everyone naturally stinks at keeping all those rules.

How do these dilemmas create roadblocks to church attendance? Well, the first dilemma—understanding that *I* stink—can keep me buried in feelings of inadequacy. The prevailing mindset may be *I can never live up to those standards; I stink too bad.* An individual can get the feeling that he has nothing of any value to offer God or the church. He may not know how to act in a church setting. Past failures may promote feelings of discouragement and uselessness. A person may feel like his résumé is not even worthy of God's glance.

Fortunately, God is more into *future* than he is into *past.* I remember a conversation I had with my wife about the future of our family. Whereas I *kind of* wanted a second dog but knew that circumstances wouldn't permit, she *really* wanted one no matter what. Her desire prompted her to ask me if I thought we could get a new puppy for Jenna to play with. I knew it was not a good time, with apartment living, but no just seemed so harsh. So I used the typical debate etiquette of coming up with an excuse. "It would be great if we could, honey," I told her, "but with our jobs neither of us can stay home to potty train a new puppy." I shrugged my shoulders fake disappointedly. "Sorry," I said, confident in my bulletproof argument.

But the conversation didn't stop there, as I had planned. Danielle, who happens to be some kind of dog encyclopedia, told me about a housebreaking technique called *crating*. Apparently, the first thing the mother dog teaches her new puppies is not to poop or pee in the place where they sleep. As a result, this knowledge is nearly instinctual for the pup. So with a new puppy, if you make it sleep in a small dog carrier (a crate) at night, it registers that place as the bed, and it won't poop or pee there. Obviously, you have to take it right outside in the morning so it realizes the right place to go potty. If you keep that puppy in the crate during the day, it will generally hold its poop and pee until you get home and again take the puppy out. Crating builds on what the puppy already knows. Pretty soon, the dog will realize that the entire apartment is a no-poop-and-pee zone.

When my wife explained this to me, I was impressed with her knowledge and disappointed that my excuse didn't seem to hold water. We tabled the whole second-dog idea for a while—but it was inevitable that we would pick it up again in the future.

God wants each person to be a part of his organization. He is willing to take what we know right now and build on it, just like crating builds on the puppy's limited knowledge. You may not know how to behave in church or what you're supposed to do, but you do know that step one is to get off the couch and walk your feet through the church door. God will begin to show you what else you need to know, and some of his experienced workers can probably help. God doesn't turn us away on the basis of our track record. He is always seeking for another willing "puppy" to bring home. Nobody stinks too bad for him.

Stinky We?

The second dilemma occurs once you actually walk through the doors of the church building. You find that the church itself is not odor free—no church is. There are people there that carry a smell indicative of their past or current failures. Not only do I stink, but at one point or another, everyone does. So many times people totally discount the church institution on the basis of those emitting the smell. No, no church is perfect, but are we naïve enough to believe that it should be? The church carries a distinct humanesque odor because it is filled with imperfect humans. This smell is not an indication of God's failure; it is an indication of his willingness to accept those of us who have failed.

Many people have had negative church experiences and as a result have decided to abandon the church system altogether. They smell a stench and assume it is God or the church system instead of the true culprit, the human factor. The system itself is God-ordained; it is the humans that have generated the failures. The church system, God's organization, remains a valuable gift no matter how we might misuse it.

As sort of a science experiment, and partially to get a reaction from Danielle, I once gave Jenna a not-so-valuable gift: a crinkled one-dollar bill. I told Jenna she could do whatever she wanted with her dollar. She decided to sniff it first, and then to lick it a little. But she quickly lost interest and left it wadded up in the living room. I grabbed it and jammed it in her collar for her. She scratched her neck with her back paw and knocked it out, and I found it lying on the floor again. I kept pushing the issue, and the dollar eventually disappeared. Danielle is the primary suspect. But the point is that Jenna had something of value, and although she didn't take care of it well, it still retained its value in her stinky paws.

Historically, we may have stunk up God's organization pretty good, yet it still retains its value. Jenna's dollar is still worth a dollar no matter what she does to it. She is just not a very good keeper of the dollar, just like some people are not very good keepers of the church or the rules. If we are looking for a good church, we must first expect a little bit of a smell indicative of humans. But we must also look for a church that is embracing their role as keeper of a very special gift. The church is something to be treasured, not endured, and the right church will reflect this attitude. We don't go to church to commiserate about our stenches; we go to church for help getting cleaned up. Because every church is not the right church, there are some important considerations to be made in choosing a church.

The first consideration is how the church makes you feel. It doesn't sound too deep or spiritual, but if you go into a church, you should feel warmth and acceptance. You shouldn't go to a church that makes you feel miserable all the time. The church you choose should fit your personality, with people, music, and preaching that you can enjoy. One of the biggest reasons I did not like church when I was younger was because I only went to the ones my parents forced me into. There was nothing wrong with these churches; they fit the bill for many types of personalities. They had great people there, but overall, they just didn't fit *my* style.

Feelings are not everything; they are only *part* of the church equation. The second consideration in choosing a church is at the opposite end of the spectrum from feelings. The right church must have sound, unwavering, time-tested principles—the ones that give evidence of God's long-term involvement. If a church is based on the right viewpoint of God, it will stand the test of time. While new music and styles are fully acceptable, new doctrine should be heavily scrutinized and, in most cases, rejected. Long ago God gave the church the keys to a connection with him. These keys are important for the church to remember and maintain; the church foundations should *not* change with the times. God's principles are not optional or wavering.

There is a balance in choosing a church. If I only went to a church that made me feel good, I would leave at the first light irritation I felt. If I only went to a church that held every ancient Christian tradition in the book, I just couldn't identify. A church should make a person feel good, but it also should be built on the pursuit of God's principles. When our feelings and God's principles clash, we already know who is right. The right church acknowledges that clash with the goal, like God's, of making better people. I don't want to be the person I used to be because that person was not very successful at all. God's plan is to take us from our solo operations as failures and turn us into successes only possible through connection with him and others. It doesn't matter where you start; only where you finish is important to God. It's okay if you stink, just so long as you realize that now it is bath time.

We've all failed. We've all done wrong. We all have a distinct human odor. But we also have a chance—an opportunity—to be part of something greater. We all have the right to grab hold of success. Granted, we might have to redefine "success" by God's terms (which is the true definition). We might have to roll up our sleeves and do some work on ourselves. But if anyone can take failure and turn it into success, if anyone can make us better people, it is God. If any system can clean us up, it must be God's program, rules and all. And the way to initiate his faith program is the same as it has always been. All we have to do is take action.

> But if wicked people turn away from all their sins and begin to obey my decrees and do what is just and right, they will surely live and not die. All their past sins will be forgotten, and they will live because of the righteous things they have done.
>
> Ezekiel 18:21-22 (NLT)

Deeper Waters

The church carries the smell of people but the providence of God. As history has proven, this is not just some fly-by-night operation. God has given us the support we need to feel loved. He has given us the regulations we need to be a continual success. Both can be found in the church, which has been time tested and has helped to preserve this "God movement" for thousands of years. If God is behind something, it is going to be huge and it is going to be unstoppable. The organization that he manages, the church collective, is both.

When we look at large, successful organizations in the business world, we see some key traits that have contributed to this lasting success. Structure is number one. Without structure, it is impossible to manage a large number of employees. There is not just one big boss over a large company; there are directors and administrators and managers and supervisors all the way up and down the ladder. The big boss might be a brilliant man or woman, but without the proper structure, that brilliance cannot be fully leveraged. There has to be a hierarchy—a chain of command.

Here again we have a tendency to hold the church up to different structural standards than the business world. God is the big boss, no doubt, but there are massive levels of confusion when it comes to any hierarchy he has established here on earth. We like to pretend that church is supposed to be a politically correct democracy, and many churches evolve in this direction. This shouldn't be.

Politically correct implies that all behaviors are accepted and tolerated. If someone is in the wrong, perhaps it is just "their way of doing it." This viewpoint is counterproductive for both the structure and moral foundation of the church, just like it is in any organization. I worked at a McDonald's restaurant for three and a half years when I was younger, and I can tell you exactly what would have happened if I decided that making Big Macs with tartar sauce (instead of Big Mac sauce) was "my way of doing it." I would have been shuffled right out the door, no questions asked. McDonald's does not retain their strength by letting employees do whatever they want. The workers have to follow protocol or the company does not achieve their customer satisfaction goals.

There is a smart way of doing things and a dumb way of doing things (and a million ways in between). God's way is the smart way. If my way is dumb, someone needs to tell me, correct me, and get me closer in line with the smart way. If I continue on the dumb path, I hurt both myself and the organization, even if the reason I am allowed to continue is dubbed "political correctness" or "tolerance." The church sometimes gets a bad rep for being intolerant, but any well-run organization reprimands or even fires those employees not operating up to standard. To continually allow unacceptable behavior hurts the entire organization.

To say that the church should be a democracy can be equally hurtful. How many human votes does it take to cancel out one of God's votes? There is no amount. If God makes it clear that something is wrong, humans cannot change it with a majority decision. The church is structured in a way that should give each person value but not necessarily the same power. The new guy on the job does not get to make decisions at the level of a company president or a manager. To do so would be foolish. So many times people come into the church smelling figuratively awful but still thinking their opinion should be highly valued and respected right off the bat. When it is not immediately accepted, they are offended and often gone.

The Lake!

I remember the first time we took Jenna to my grandma's cottage on Hubbard Lake. That's right, a lake. Jenna had never seen such a huge water bowl in all her life. It was hot that day, so Danielle and I decided to go for a swim. As we paddled around out by the end of the dock, we noticed Jenna looking on longingly from shore.

"C'mon Jenna," Danielle said, coaxing her. Jenna trotted into the water up to her chest and then became apprehensive. This wasn't just walking through the plain old air anymore; the water created uncomfortable resistance. Jenna glanced back at the shore.

We could see we were losing her, so we began to encourage the pup. "Come on out, girl!" I called. "Come see Mommy and Daddy!"

She looked again and remembered how much she liked "her parents." Boldness swept over her, and she plodded out deeper until only her head was above water. She stopped again.

I wonder what was going on in her brain. She was definitely uncertain, yet she saw Mommy and Daddy swimming and playing and apparently having fun. Swimming looked easy enough to her, but she was still nervous about the plunge. We didn't let her think long before we gave her another barrage of encouragement.

"Come here, Jenna. C'mon, you can do it."

That last prompting was all she needed to forget her worries for a second and head out into deeper waters. But her worries came rushing back when she realized there was no longer ground under her feet—just water. She spazzed out! She ferociously began pounding the water with her front paws, trying to keep her head high above the water as her back half began to sink. Next thing we knew, she was virtually vertical in the water, with her head straight up, front paws thrashing, and a look of terror in her eyes. Her mind was frantically racing to tap into that instinct that told her how to keep her body afloat. Swimming certainly wasn't as easy as Mommy and Daddy had made it look!

Jenna got herself turned back around and slowly flailed her way to the shallow water. Once safe, she began to gaze out at us with those sad, puppy-dog eyes, again wishing she could join us.

When we compare me and God, we can clearly see that he outranks me. When we start to compare me and other workers in God's organization, it is quite clear that many of them outrank me as well. In the deep things of God, they are far more proficient "swimmers" than I am. This can be especially true of the pastors, priests, and ministers but extends to any respected mentor or pillar within the church. Not only are they superior in their understandings of God, but they are often working to coax me into deeper waters. Sometimes in this effort they are exposing my shortcomings and making me uncomfortable. Sometimes they are prodding me to do things I am not sure about. Why are they so incessant in their encouragements?

The same reason I was relentless in my coaxing of Jenna. Because I knew it would be better for her. Jenna was a little nervous about the huge lake, especially after her first swimming episode. But she didn't give up, and neither did I. I kept encouraging her. I went in to shore to pet her. I even picked the big galoot up and helped her ease into the deeper water. It was tough for her, but you know what? Now she *loves* the water! The lake is her favorite place to go. She will play fetch in the water until she is dead tired and wheezing from exhaustion. I can throw the tennis ball as far as I like out into the water, and she will faithfully retrieve it.

It's funny because many times when we go up to the lake on holiday weekends like the Fourth of July, there will be another family in a cottage close by with a yellow Lab named Angel. She is a little smaller than Jenna, but they are pretty much clones of each other, appearance-wise. The main difference between them is that Angel is still scared of the water. She won't go over her head. But she watches Jenna chase the ball out into the lake. Angel slowly gets bolder and bolder with each throw and has been known to have a few flailing moments of her own. Having Jenna beside her, leading the way, encourages Angel to push out into deeper waters. Someday they will both be swimming around together.

God has some example people out there for us so that we can push out deeper in our knowledge of him. Some of these examples are normal churchgoers, and some of them are on church staff. We need to understand the incredible importance of these people for our lives. If we stick around them, we will be encouraged to move closer to the place God wants us.

God can change history with earthquakes or lightning bolts. He could protect the church by sending fire down from heaven on all of its naysayers and enemies. But he doesn't usually choose this route. He chooses to preserve and protect the church by raising up a structure headed by pastors and priests. He puts people in charge who can lead the rest of the people to safety. God does his work through people. And if you get in the right church and pay special attention, you can see the people God is working through. You can see the people whose lives and attitudes seem to be constantly getting better. Follow them!

> He is the one who gave these gifts to the church: the apostles, the prophets, the evangelists, and the pastors and teachers. Their responsibility is to equip God's people to do his work and build up the church...
>
> Ephesians 4:11-12 (NLT)

Part 4:

God and the Individual: The Importance of the Bible

God the Friend

I need Jenna to see me as her president, "king" over the realm she inhabits. I require her to understand that I am her boss. These are prerequisites before the connection can go any further. If Jenna will not respect and obey me to the best of her ability, then we are stuck on the preliminary steps, never to go beyond. There is a legitimate question as to whether we can ever become closer if she remains disobedient. It might look like rules and regulations to Jenna, some annoying, but the payout is coexistence and safety.

You see, the strength of the connection I have with Jenna is not in the rules I impose on her. It isn't in a growing list of commandments dictating her every movement. The very reason I seek to have a connection with the dog is so that we can play together and be together. I don't love the rules; I love the dog. I want Jenna to live a wonderful life, and I want to be a part of that life. As my connection with Jenna strengthens, it becomes more of an actual relationship with the pup. In this relationship we really begin to understand each other better.

God's main goal is not to be a hard boss, like so many of us view him. His goal is instead to build relationships with human beings, collectively and individually. This relationship has purpose, therefore there are requirements. God doesn't want to be simply a Sunday-morning acquaintance. God's requirements create their own benefits, such as structure and discipline, but the ultimate payout is the relationship developed with the one who designed the requirements. When we develop a relationship with God, we begin to see the hidden value of the many regulations—how they help both individuals and God's organization.

If we can't see around God's position of authority over us to his heart that desires a strengthening connection, then we will never develop more than a work relationship with him. A work relationship is beneficial, but it can be boring, which is another common complaint against the church scene. If church seems boring, it certainly isn't God's fault. This boredom may be an indication that we know God's authority but don't understand his friendship (or that particular church doesn't understand it). In this case, we need to invest some of our work ethic in getting to know God as a friend, not just in getting out of bed Sunday morning.

I wrote earlier about the first time Jenna and I met. She only had to do a few seconds of sniffing before she decided she wanted to be my buddy. She barreled out of Danielle's apartment and slammed into me with a contagious joy that made us fast friends. I absolutely love that greeting, and I get it most every time I enter the apartment door today. What a welcome!

Jenna's reaction is similar to the way some people react to God. A few minutes of religious education—sniffing around—and they can clearly see that God is the one for them. Their excitement is uncontainable as they gladly greet their new pal. Emotions flood through them as they realize what a great friend they have in God; they cry, they laugh, they rejoice. I have to believe that God enjoys this display.

Other people, like myself, tend to need a whole lot more sniffing before they are willing to greet a new president or boss. These people want to get all the facts so they can make an educated decision about who God is and what benefits he provides. Once all the pieces are in place, then there is opportunity for the development of a friendship and beyond. The structure of this book follows my sniffing pattern.

There is nothing wrong with either approach to befriending God. We should be joyful to know we are in such good hands, but we should also become well educated about our heavenly friend. Only when one of these aspects is neglected is there danger of relational damage.

If, for example, the exuberant believer—the easily excitable—does not build on the foundation of joy by using that energy to advance his or her knowledge of God, then the excitement may fizzle. Getting close to God has to be more than just a temporary feeling. Certainly God enjoys our friendship, but we also must appropriately respect him as superior. If Jenna was always happy to see me but never obeyed me, we would have a big problem, and coexistence would be a challenge.

On the other hand, if the over-analyzing type does not move beyond seeing God as a boss, then he or she may work with the church diligently for a lifetime and never see any spiritual advancement. God is much deeper than just his ability to direct. He wants us to have an emotional connection to him. He enjoys relationships just like we humans do. He isn't looking for unfeeling robots. He certainly has the technology to make those if he wants. I would love for Jenna to be ultra-obedient, but I wouldn't sacrifice all of her excitement for it.

Here again, balance is the key. God needs to be our boss, and he wants to be our friend. Our neglect of either role will result in a stunted relationship—a connection that is less than it should be. For me personally, I knew I was heavy on the analytical side and light on the friendship. I had to do a little soul searching, as the pursuit of God frequently requires. I wanted to understand why I tended to have more of a challenging time developing a friendship with God. I hoped that discovering the root of my struggle would aid in my victory and a deeper relationship with God.

Hidden Damage

I once had a friend who had a pit bull named Ashley. Pit bulls are known for their aggression, of course, but Ashley was a sweet little pup. Instead of showing any malevolence toward people, Ashley respected them greatly. She would gingerly come up to me, trying not to be too forward, but unable to resist an opportunity to be petted. When I reached out my hand, she would cower at first and then accept the attention. I wasn't particularly big on dogs at the time, but I enjoyed Ashley's demeanor. I did wonder why she was so hesitant.

Then the answer came. Ashley's owner, it seems, was prone to fits of pit-bull-like aggression himself. During these fits he would badly mistreat her to the point that she feared him. His anger became one of her sole motivations for behaving. They say that most pit bulls eventually turn on their masters. In this case, if it ever happened, I can't really say that I would blame the dog.

As I mentioned before, I was raised in a Christian home, but no child is immune to the abuses of real life. I had a great connection with both of my parents, and, including my two sisters, we were one big, happy, cohesive family unit. That was, until my parents decided to get a divorce when I was in grade school. I was absolutely crushed, completely unaware that there had been any problem at all. I had thought everything was perfect, and then I found out how wrong I had apparently been. The pain of this event sent ripples deep into my future.

I had some crying nights and sad times in the weeks and months that followed my parents' announcement, but I eventually got better. At least on the surface. I continued to perform well in school, trusting in logic and analysis to get me through the years. But on the inside, where I carried my true pain, I was like an abused pit bull. I logically knew how to submit to authority, and "play their game," so to speak. But the emotional trauma of the divorce had effectively stunted my ability to build connections with people—to make friends. Internally, I cowered at the thought of investing my emotions in anybody. Yet on the surface, I seemed fine and had a number of peers I hung around with regularly. Inside, I had the toughest time actually connecting with them. I just felt like I couldn't trust anyone. As I got older, this damage continued to grow inside me.

The authoritative system was my master, and I continued to submit as necessary. Subconsciously, however, I was waiting for my opportunity to turn on this master. With independence from my parents, I had my chance to attack the system that confined me, and I did so with my rebellious lifestyle. That rebellion landed me in the addictive, depressive mess I was in when I started looking for God. Like Ashley, I knew how to submit. But inside I didn't know how to build a friendship very well anymore.

When I started seeking God, and I began to understand a little bit about him, I made the logical choice to submit. Submitting I could do—I was well versed in that department. But I soon realized that God wanted more from me. He wanted to be my boss *and* my friend. He wanted to be more than just rules and regulations to me, which is how I was conditioned to perceive him. I had taken the aspect of God that I understood, his authority, and blown it way out of proportion. I fully grasped the fact that God could crush me if he wanted, so I lived in a sort of fear of him. But this fear was only the beginning of the wisdom I needed to grow closer to God (Psalm 111:10).

The church helped me to develop some basic understandings about God—specifically his superiority, authority, and structure. I eventually became a regular attendee. Just hanging around helped me draw closer to God. Consequently, with nine months of positive support and education provided by the church, I finally kicked both the drug and alcohol habits for good. Things were looking up. My pursuit of God had proven to me that each step closer to him created benefits in my life, which my analytical nature appreciated. I was better off, but my life still didn't feel 100 percent fulfilled. My logical conclusion? Keep pressing closer to God.

It occurred to me that God must want me to know him better. My preliminary steps had been rewarding, and my life was on a better track. If God wanted to simply hide in the background of human life, he could. If he wanted to be big and bold on the scene, flying across the skies in extraordinary displays of his power, he could do that too. But he has chosen somewhere in the middle—a place where we have to search, but we will find. He must want us to search—to *work* to get closer to him. So I expanded my search and began to get serious about reading the church-acclaimed Bible.

In the Bible, I found a God of judgment and justice, no doubt. The Old Testament has many stories about God's rules and the capital punishment that disobedience often incurred. But I also started to notice that there was a connection God had with many of the biblical characters, like with Abraham and David and Peter. I started to see God's desire to have a deepening connection with us and, more specifically, me (there's that practical applicability). Our role is to accept the friendship he is offering us. He wants us to be his friend, so if we are not, then we are doing the opposite of what he wants. We are moving away from the source of the good things in life.

God has designed beacons for us to help us know that he exists. He has provided ways for us to comprehend his authority. And he has given us paths so that we can develop our connection with him. For us, to take these paths is only logical. God wants us to be his friends. The closer we get to God, the better our lives will get.

> But seek ye first the kingdom of God, and his righteousness; and all these things shall be added unto you.
>
> Matthew 6:33 (KJV)

The Manual that Overrides

God knows everything there is to know about our universe, our solar system, our planet, our countries, our cities, and even us individually. He is an expert in human psychology, which is one of the most mysterious human studies. I can't even figure out how my own mind works (or doesn't work) sometimes. What a challenge it is to understand the human animal. A challenge, that is, for humans.

God knows how our brains function and what tendencies are rooted deep within our subconscious. Our physical, mental, emotional, and spiritual needs are not mysterious to him, and he is quite willing to provide for them. We've already talked about man's communal nature, how we tend to run with a pack, and how God has supplied for this need with the church. But humankind's needs are not met simply by a building or a group of people. God knows we are deeper than that. Most of us, myself included, are not very good at operating on "blind faith." We need intellectual reinforcement if we are going to believe anything, at least initially. We need to understand procedures step by step before we are willing to put a foot forward.

Wal-Mart Knows

When I go to Wal-Mart and buy a shelving unit in a box, I understand that there will be assembly required. I understand that my gender is renowned for our disregard of directions, but not me. I'm not a handyman at all—just ask my father-in-law. If I'm buying a shelf, it had better darn well have some instructions in it, or I will be building a loosely connected stack of boards. Those instructions must be very simple, or I won't be able to get the job done.

Now if the executives at Wal-Mart can figure out that the customer needs instructions with their assembly-required purchases, certainly God can grasp the concept. If there is construction to be done in my life, developing my relationship with God, it only makes sense that God provide some tangible instruction that I can follow. I need more than church theory and doctrine; I need something I can hold in my hands. If I have the instructions, I can get the job done.

As I began to read the Bible more, I started to realize that God *does* provide instructions for mankind. Contained in that ancient book are hints, illustrations, and even direct insights into the personality of God. No doubt it isn't the easiest reading, and it can be challenging to understand. But it contains key directions on how to live life in a way that will bring us closer to God. God saw that we needed written instructions—something to hold on to—so he provided us with the Bible. I might not be a biblical handyman quite yet, but I know how to read and follow directions. Fortunately this quaint ability can help bring me closer to the God who can reconstruct anything, especially broken lives.

I am well aware of the fact that a great deal of skepticism surrounds the Bible; I originally had it myself. The concept of God is relatively easy to accept, especially here in America. But an ancient book that supposedly contains the secrets of God's personality may seem a little far-fetched. The Bible has amazing literary value and completeness for its age, scholars will agree, but its spiritual value is highly debated. While man's need for instructions may answer the *why* element of the Bible, questions as to its reliability may shake people's trust in the book. Perhaps God did ordain its writing thousands of years ago, but it may seem very unlikely that any ancient manuscript could pass through man's hands without a severe level of data corruption. This is especially true in the case of a religiously charged document such as the Bible. So how reliable is this ancient book?

Divine Protection

As I mentioned earlier, I got into an accident driving to work years ago. Going well over the fifty-five-miles-per-hour speed limit, I swerved to miss a deer and wound up cutting the wheel on my SUV too sharply. Before I knew what was going on, the truck was rolling. It made two complete revolutions, blowing the windows out and totaling the truck's body, before it finally came to rest just beyond the ditch in someone's driveway. The telephone pole or any one of the pine trees nearby could have ended the rolling and my life prematurely. It was an exciting ride, to say the least.

A quick analysis of my physical condition after the accident showed that I was in perfect health. I had a few cuts, but nothing more. In a classic post-trauma maneuver, I thanked God for keeping me safe through this death-defying adventure that had lasted only seconds. I probably hadn't thought about God for weeks or months before that.

I was quick to credit God with my protection for my rollover accident. I truly believe he watched over me while this danger surrounded me. He has the power to protect. But so often we limit this power to a matter of seconds or minutes. We ask God for protection through a difficult time or protection for our family or friends when they are away from home. There is nothing wrong with asking for this, but we need to realize that God can preserve us through far more than just a dangerous time. With his help, we can survive all sorts of disasters for our entire lives on planet earth.

So the question is, why couldn't God do the same with an ancient manuscript? Why couldn't he preserve the Bible throughout the dangerous ages that it was in man's hands? To say God couldn't do this questions his power. He saw our need for instructions, and he came through for us. We don't have to operate completely on theory or blindly because we have a great deal of truth at our disposal in the form of the Bible. If God can preserve me for a few seconds, he can preserve the Bible for as long as he has to. Since he is all powerful, this isn't too hard to believe.

It is a well-known fact that the Bible is the most published book on earth. Is this a fluke or perhaps simply randomness? No; like the church, God is operating in history's defining moments. He is actively at work preserving those things he deems most important. He wants to sustain for us an environment in which we can choose him—choose to be his friend. The Bible gives us insight into how that amazing process takes place. If you prefer historical narratives illustrating who God is, the Bible has them. If you prefer snippets of information about wisdom and praise, the Bible has them. If you prefer teachings directly from the mouths and pens of God's chosen ancient pastors and priests, the Bible has them. God knows just what we need to grow into a full relationship with him, and he isn't going to withhold it. Written instruction fulfills one of these needs.

Growing Up and Out

Jenna doesn't wear clothing too often—it is not one of her needs. When Jenna was a puppy, my wife got her the cutest little bumblebee outfit. I'm not sure if Jenna appreciated the cuteness, but Mommy sure did. It is very hard to make a little yellow Lab puppy any cuter, but this outfit did it. And from time to time, Mommy and Daddy still get a kick out of throwing a pirate costume on her for Halloween or a shepherd outfit for Christmas card pictures. Despite Jenna's affinity toward prancing around in the buff, she still has to put up with a little costume fun on occasion.

It would be adorable if we could get the bumblebee costume out and stick Jenna in it for old time's sake, but there's a little problem. That problem is about seventy extra pounds of dog. Jenna obviously can no longer fit into her childhood clothing, which is why we have to come up with the new stuff. Growing up (and filling out) is natural and healthy for any living being.

Like Jenna, we all have some growing to do, especially as it relates to our relationship with God. Whatever our level of knowledge is, from uneducated to highly educated, the Bible always has something that fits our ability. God always knows exactly how to communicate at our level. The Bible is a big book, but there are a lot of levels God wants to reach with it, and there are a lot of instructions he wants to convey. The more complicated the project, the more complex the instructions must be. God has supplied us with a masterpiece of instruction to help us tackle the challenging project of continual growth.

People trust in books all the time. If we have a problem, we look to self-help books. If we want to understand history or science or math, we get a book and believe what we read. If we need entertainment, we often look to books (though that trend is diminishing). It only makes sense that if we want to know God better, we trust in the book that speaks of him—the book that he has ordained to be in our hands.

> All Scripture is inspired by God and is useful to teach us what is true and to make us realize what is wrong in our lives. It straightens us out and teaches us to do what is right.
>
> 2 Timothy 3:16 (NLT)

Hearing Repaired

Jenna's affinity toward food has always been a trouble spot in her obedience. We keep her treats in a ceramic dog-house-shaped cookie jar, and she certainly knows it. One afternoon while Mommy and Daddy were at work, Jenna began to plot against the treat jar. It might have been behind a few things on the counter, a bit of a challenge to access, but not impossible for a resourceful thinker like her. Heck, she had the entire workday to burn. How exactly she accomplished the task is still a bit of a mystery, but when we got home from work, there was her treat jar sitting on the floor, virtually unharmed. It was also virtually empty.

When I arrived at home and saw the jar, I told Jenna, "No! *Bladu baba nunu goo godga glastobule*!" Well, that's not really what I said, but that's what she heard. One word she recognized—the *no*. The rest was just mindless, angry gibberish. Still, she had heard the piece she needed and headed to her pout spot. Because of our brief "conversation," she understood that discretionary consumption of her doggy treats was unacceptable.

Based on her understanding of a single English word, Jenna slowly began to realize that the words pouring out of my mouth were more than just background noise. In fact, the next time she violated the treat-jar rule, she heard, "No! *Bladu baba nunu goo* treats *glastobule*!" Treats. It seemed to her that she had heard that word before—but when was it? Oh, yes, it was when the master held one of those yum yums and said a bunch of other stuff. Jenna realized that the yum yums must be called *treats*. She promptly made a mental note to listen for that word. Now, anytime I say *treats*, Jenna's ears perk up, and her eyes bug out. *Is he talking about yum yums?*

Jenna came to understand that there is meaning and purpose to the words that I speak. Not only do these words scold, but they can also convey very important messages—the top of the important list being treats, of course. She started listening harder, and can now recognize phrases like "go out," "go potty," and "go for ride." Her English comprehension went from zero words to one word (with the help of a painful swat), and then from one word to probably around twenty with the help of regular repetition and a little treat-induced attentiveness on her part. Now Jenna understands me far better than before, and our relationship is improved because of it. Jenna's life is improved because of it.

God has an incredible store of wisdom for us as well—information designed to improve our lives. That information is contained chiefly in the words of the Bible. And while it seems like having an accessible Bible would theoretically turn a person's life around, we often run into comprehension problems similar to Jenna's. I know that's the problem I ran into when I began regularly reading my Bible. I would read a passage, and all I would get out of it was "Bladu baba nunu goo godga glastobule." Very little of what the Bible said made a whole lot of sense to me, yet I knew it was important to try to understand God's words, and ultimately to understand him better.

So with the help of regular repetition, I began to pick a little bit more out of the Bible than just the "thou shalt nots." Words started to catch my attention—words such as *love* and *peace* and *joy*. The Bible is peppered with them. I wanted these things in my life, but my track record had proven that I didn't know how to get them. Sure, I had tried to break into the treat jar to get these things illegitimately, but my efforts were unfulfilling at best. I began to understand that the Bible—God's words—provided instructions for legitimately obtaining those intangibles for which I had been searching. My ears started to perk up. I started listening. And I found that, like Jenna, my comprehension could be improved.

But comprehension is not the only problem encountered in reading the Bible. In fact, comprehension turns out to be the least of our problems once we apply ourselves to listening. God's words meet us where we are at; the novice reader and the decorated scholar can both draw personally applicable truths from the Bible. If effort is applied, any and every person can develop an understanding of what God is saying. The problem often becomes actually applying that effort.

It would seem to me that if I, the keeper of the treats, speak to Jenna, the eater of the treats, she would want to listen every time. But it doesn't always work this way. Sometimes she doesn't want to apply the effort to listen to me. When does this occur? Usually when she already has a treat or a bone. Once she is satisfied, she has a tendency to neglect me. She doesn't care what I say if she is working on devouring a bone. Oftentimes, she only comes to me when she wants something. As soon as she has it, she runs off. This is not how a friendship should work.

We do the same thing with God sometimes. We are only willing to listen to his words when we want something from him. Struggles arise, and suddenly we are devout in our Bible reading and prayer. Once the storm passes, we go back to our way of doing things until it fails again, and then back to God with a listening ear. Maybe this approach works with a distant president, but if we want to advance our relationship with God, we cannot be only a fair-weather friend. True friendship doesn't take days off. We must have a listening ear toward God during the good times and the bad. If we will only listen during the tough times, then tough times are what he will supply us.

Warmth-Filled Words

In a typical day, I will greet Jenna with a hearty "How's my puppy?" I usually follow that up with, "You's a good dog, aren't you? What a good girl. What a pretty puppy dog." Of course, I am petting her belly the whole time, and she is just eating this greeting up. I continue to heap compliments upon her as her squinty-eyed Lab smile radiates with enjoyment. All morning, as my wife and I prepare for work, we constantly saturate Jenna with kind words.

So given Jenna's very limited English comprehension, are Danielle and I nuts? Are we crazy for continually speaking to a languageless animal? Some may say yes, but I'll bet those are the people who do not own pets. Anyone who has owned a dog or cat or hamster has probably fallen into the same single-sided conversational habit. No matter what animals can or cannot understand, we as human masters love to talk to our pets. We have a lot that we would like to communicate with them.

Certainly the words I use have meaning, most of which Jenna will never comprehend. But the most important message I am trying to convey is not the words specifically. I want Jenna to hear my *tone*. I want her to understand that she is the focus of my good intentions. I believe that the best way to elevate our connection is for her to realize how much I care, not for her to increase her vocabulary a hundredfold. I want her to know by my words that I love her, even if the word definitions themselves fall upon deaf ears.

God knows that the book he has provided is big and complex to us. He doesn't expect us to understand everything in it, especially in the early going. What he does want is for us to hear his tone. He wants us to realize that the Bible is a message from a heavenly friend to an earthly one—you—and it is intended to communicate God's care. Sure, he wants us to up our listening and eventually our biblical vocabulary, but if we do not understand that his intentions for us are friendly, he would be disappointed. If we only see God as a boss, his words might sound bossy to us. If we see him as a good-intentioned friend, suddenly his advice has increasing value.

God is speaking to humanity, and more specifically to you, through the Bible. He wants his words to give us hope and guidelines to get from Point A to Point B. But more than that, he wants to let us know how much he cares about us, much like I do with my affirming words for Jenna. Throughout the Bible, there is so much encouragement for those who have chosen to be on God's side. God tells us he will never leave us or forsake us (Hebrews 13:5). He tells us he knew us before we were born (Jeremiah 1:5). He tells us that he calls us friends, contingent in part on our obedience (John 15:14). And the list goes on. I never noticed what a caring guy he is until I started to move past the dictator stereotype.

We can let encouraging words like these roll off our backs, like Jenna does when she is preoccupied with eating or playing, or we can take them to heart. We can see that God has more than just wrath to pour out on the people of the earth. He wants a connection that develops into a relationship and keeps on developing after that. Though he knows we have trouble hearing him, he isn't speaking just to hear himself talk. He is expressing that he is a caring friend to us. And as they say, friendship is a two-way street. It doesn't work unless both parties are willing.

The Hunger for Truth

If Jenna decides that her sole motivation for greeting me is food, I can't stop her. It would hurt me to know this, but Jenna certainly has the option to live her life from bowlful to bowlful. The thing is, I have so much more for her. Food might pacify her, but it does not fulfill her desire for companionship. Food cannot take the place of my encouraging words. If Jenna was totally deprived of human contact, her life would not be full. She would live uninspired. Because she has developed a healthy dependence on my friendship—on my words—her life is about more than just the physical world. She has a natural hunger for food, but a developed hunger for my friendship.

How many times do we go through days and weeks with a full belly but totally uninspired? The physical world can supply some needs, but not all of them. If we want to live a vibrant, excited life, we have to feed off the energy—the care—God is sending our way. I really had to work on it, but I eventually developed a hunger for what God says, a hunger for the words of the Bible. It is a healthy dependence to have, unlike many of our other dependencies. We will never feel complete if we do not listen to God, and we may never know the depth of God's love if we fail to heed his written words. Each one of us needs his or her spirit lifted from time to time, so we need to get some spiritual food into our minds and heart. God supplies completeness a whole lot better than the supermarket can.

> Man does not live on bread alone but on every word that comes from the mouth of the Lord.
>
> Deuteronomy 8:3b (NIV)

> The words I have spoken to you are spirit and they are life.
>
> John 6:63b (NIV)

> He that hath an ear, let him hear what the Spirit saith unto the churches.
>
> Revelation 2:29 (KJV)

The Lame Name

I know we're far past the first-impression stage of this book, but let me ask you a question. What do you think about the name "Jenna" for a dog? My initial thought was that Jenna is a people name—kind of silly for an animal. Of course, I wasn't even in the picture when Danielle named the pup, so I couldn't give my input. In fact, Jenna's full name is actually Jenna Juliette because my wife couldn't choose between these two gems. "Juliette" got second place because Danielle thought it would be a little weird calling for the dog: "Juliette! Juliette! Wherefore art thou, Juliette?" Fortunately I'm on a first-name basis with Jenna, so I don't ever have to use her Shakespearian name.

Nowadays, when I look at Jenna, I realize that Danielle was right on with that name. The dog looks like a Jenna to me now. While I may have once used that name with uncertainty, I now affectionately call my dog Jenna. And Jenna responds to that name. When she is straying, she returns at the call of her name…at least 70 percent of the time. Jenna is forever attached to her name; there is no changing it now. She may have been born a blank slate, but she is now Jenna until the day she dies. She is stuck on who she is.

Have you ever looked at someone and thought, *That guy just looks like a Bill? Or maybe Jerry or Tom?* Sometimes it seems like a person somehow matches a name perfectly. In fact, most people, once you get to know them, seem to fit nicely with their names. When a man introduces himself, I accept the name he gives me. I don't argue that he has his name all wrong because he looks to me like a Todd or a Joe. There is an automatic and natural association of a person with his or her name. Though each of us was born nameless, we now answer to the name given us by our parents.

So here is a personal question: Have you ever looked at someone and thought, *That guy looks like a loser*? Or perhaps *a druggie*, or just *a jerk*? If we're being truthful, I have to admit that I have. We might accept a person's name, but at the same time we often assign them a label. That label can be extremely hard to dissociate—for the labeler *and* for the labelee. If everyone believes that I am a loser, I might start to believe it too. Winning will become that much more difficult for me if I adopt the label given me by those around me.

I used to have a nickname back in my partying days: Clay-Stone. I'd like to say it was because of my rock-hard work ethic, or perhaps physique, but truthfully it was because I was stoned all the time. At that point in my life, I didn't mind the nickname; in fact, I embraced it. Clay was my given name, nothing wrong with it, but Clay-Stone was the person I had become. And that particular person took me down some dark paths.

So a change was eventually necessary—a change that started when I began attending church again. Things were looking up, but I just didn't feel like I was changed inside. I felt like deep down I still had that same deviant, Clay-Stone, locked away in a box, waiting to break free. I did all the internal fighting I could, but often I returned to my habits and my old self in the early going. I just couldn't change who I thought I was.

When I failed to change me, I decided to try another route. I couldn't get my rock-headed self going in the right direction, so I figured I would let God give it a shot. And as I continued in moderate Bible reading, I began to develop a deeper understanding of what

God could do with me. To myself, I may have been a loser, but to God, I was really someone special. The Bible made it clear that God could help me become a new-and-improved me.

The Bible talks about a guy named Saul. Saul wanted badly to do what God wanted him to do, but he was entirely confused. He eventually got so wrapped up in his misconceptions about God that he was actually killing and imprisoning God's true followers. To the early churches, Saul was known as a bad man. But God used a technique to "get rid" of Saul that surprised the early church.

God didn't kill Saul, as some in the church may have hoped. Instead, God took this zealous enemy and he *changed* him. God had to wake Saul up with some life-changing moments, and he also instructed him with the help of the churches and the scriptures. But the name Saul still suggested an old lifestyle of ignoring God's truth. So the simple solution? Saul changed his name to Paul. Under this name, he carried the baton of the church and wrote thirteen of the twenty-nine books of the New Testament. Once he left Saul behind, Paul could become the man God wanted him to be.

The Bible shows multiple occurrences of this renaming trend. Abram became Abraham, the father of nations. He is the Father Abraham from which the Jewish race descended. Jacob was renamed Israel, which is still a nation to this day. Simon became the Apostle Peter and along the way an emboldened preacher. In all of these instances, God had a direct hand in the changes that took place in the lives of these classic Bible characters.

The point is not that we need to go have our legal names changed once we decide to follow God, nor deny our heritages. The point is instead that we all need a change—a change that only God can complete. God didn't see Saul as Saul the persecutor, an oppressive and contrary man, although that is exactly what he was. God instead saw him as the Apostle Paul, and calls him a "chosen instrument to carry my name" (Acts 9:15, NIV). And Paul became a mighty friend of God.

I don't see my dog as plain old Jenna the weirdly named dog. I see her as Jen-Jen, my buddy, the best dog I could hope for. And God doesn't see me as Clay-Stone the stoner; he never did. He saw what I could become. He saw me as the person he could change me into. The only problem was that *I* didn't see who he could change me into—I just saw the mess I was. But then I began to read his words and understand how he had taken Joe Schmoes throughout biblical history and changed them into mighty men and women for his purposes. I didn't want to be the same old guy anymore; I wanted to be what God had planned for me. I wanted to be a new person. I knew it was possible, but only with God's help.

The Bible is the key to breaking through the world's programming. We have no control over the people giving us the labels; we can only control our subjection and reaction to the labels. If we continue to allow those negative labelers to pour into our lives, we will have no defense against the pigeonhole in which we've been placed. But if we limit our time with the negative influencers and instead consistently subject ourselves to the positive, we can overcome the stereotypes and prejudices stacked against us. The words of God—what the Bible says about you and me—are necessary in building the strongest possible defense against the world's labeling system. You might think you are nothing, but God says you are something, and he's always right. The truth will set you free from the world's grip (see John 8:32).

God has a loving name for each one of us. He has a person he wants us to become—a person only he can see right now. And he has the ability to make the necessary changes happen, just like he did with Abraham, Israel, Peter, and Paul. He wants us to see who we are to him, not who society has labeled us as. And that's why he wants us to listen to him telling us who we can become through the Bible. We don't have to be stuck on our versions of Clay-Stone forever. God can take the old and turn it into something new.

What this means is that those who become Christians become new persons. They are not the same anymore, for the old life is gone. A new life has begun!

2 Corinthians 5:17 (NLT)

To him that overcometh will I give to eat of the hidden manna, and will give him a white stone, and in the stone a new name written, which no man knoweth saving he that receiveth it.

Revelation 2:17b (KJV)

The Jenglish Language

Not many phrases strike joy and excitement into the heart of an indoor-dwelling dog than do the words, "Go out, go potty!" Often I test Jenna's super-sensitive hearing by whispering this magical phrase under my breath or from another room. She can be dead tired, even sleeping, and still her ears perk up and her eyes bug out. She looks around the room, stunned, until I whisper it again. She is on me in a flash, and I don't get a second of rest until the implied promise has been fulfilled—until we go out and she goes potty.

I don't know if Jenna has ever actually dissected this phrase, but really it has two key pieces. The first piece—"go out"—gets a rise out of her with or without the second part. "Go out" describes our exciting embarkment into the great out of doors. Outside of our apartment there are many highly rated doggie loves—smells, sounds, neighbor dogs, local wildlife, open spaces, Frisbees, tennis balls, and others. The possibilities are endless. Once we step outside the apartment, there are a million things to distract Jenna from her responsibility, the second piece of the phrase.

"Go potty" is what Jenna is supposed to do once we get outside. Sure, there are times we go out to play, but this responsibility almost always exists as a requirement of our outdoor visits. Jenna may have a goal, to have fun, but Daddy has a goal too. I know that if she does not go potty before the workday begins, she will not be able to make it all eight-plus hours inside. An accident is inevitable if

Jenna does not fulfill her responsibility. Though I cannot force her to go, I do want to give her every opportunity to avoid a connection-compromising poop.

Benefits

Everyone in the world has adopted some form of belief system, even if that system happens to be believing that nothing is worth believing. These personal belief systems generally have two primary components, much like Jenna's go-out-go-potty phrase. The first component is benefit. People typically adopt a belief system that gives them some sort of benefit, such as the promise of personal improvement. The second component of belief systems is the responsibility required to achieve this benefit. We rightfully understand that progress requires an element of effort on our behalf. Advancement cannot happen if we refuse to move.

God's system, as we've discussed, turns out to be a system of incredible benefit. Even if our goal is simply to shuck a negative label, God's system provides for this desire. The Bible is just the reprogramming we need to break free from prevailing negative mindsets. At the same time, God's system also supplies us with some very challenging responsibilities. He has goals too, and the responsibilities are intended to advance his purposes for planet earth. These often-daunting responsibilities can also be found locked away in his big instructional manual, the Bible.

The problem we encounter here is interpretation. Most people who believe in God will tell you that they believe in the Bible as well, but what does that mean? Some have never read a word of the Bible but feel that belief in the Bible is synonymous with belief in God. In other words, they believe that the message of the Bible is simply that God exists and nothing more. Other people believe in the general proverbial application of the Bible but see large portions of the text as entirely inapplicable to modern society. Still others believe in the literal interpretation of every word of the Bible, from commandments to food regulations to seemingly symbolic illustrations. Many people give up on the whole thing, citing incomprehensibility or perceived contradictions. That's definitely where I was for a while. So what is the best way to interpret the Bible? How literal is this ancient book intended to be taken?

Well, there are two key words in these questions: *best* and *intended*. First off, we must come to terms with the fact that there is a *best* way of understanding the Bible. Just like the fact that there are many views on God, there are many views about the Bible, but only one is the complete, unabated truth, which is the goal of our search. True to the complete benevolence of his character, God wants us to find this best way. In fact, the way that God *intended* the Bible to be understood is in this best way. His goal was our comprehension. God didn't assemble the Bible just to get his thoughts down on paper; God assembled the Bible specifically for us.

So when God revealed certain truths about himself to the ancient authors and when God protected his selected manuscript components over the years, did he eventually drop the ball? In his infinite power and wisdom, did he accidentally allow a bunch of inapplicable fluff into the book that best describes him? Of course not. To believe that the Bible we hold in our hands today is any different from the Bible God wanted us to have is to doubt his power. The Bible we have today is *exactly* the Bible God intended for us to have—both the benefits and the responsibilities.

Responsibilities

Back when I began seriously reading the Bible, I really didn't like much of what I read. Sure, the benefits sounded great, but the responsibilities seemed stifling. Some of the activities that had become staples of my lifestyle—drunkenness, fornication, and pridefulness, to name a few—were explicit violations of God's rules. I wished that I could remove some of those things from the Bible so that I could continue to justify my reckless behavior. But every time I tried to get away with something I knew was wrong, I felt like I was slapping God in the face. Indirectly, I was either telling him he wasn't smart enough to assemble an accurate instruction manual or that he wasn't powerful enough to preserve that manual over the years.

Even then, I assumed that one day after this lifetime I would get to meet God. If at that time he rolled a clip of me reading "you shall not lie" in the Bible and then a series of clips of me later lying my butt off, what on earth would I tell him? I would have no excuse whatsoever. The common defense, "I didn't know it was wrong," would be blown out of the water. I had clearly been told that lying was wrong by the Bible, and no amount of legal maneuvering would be able to reverse that fact. And the same is true of any of the instructions within the Bible. When we violate a clearly presented passage, we have no defense before God. We knew better but did worse.

Because the Bible is exactly the book God wants us to have, there is only one logical way of interpreting it—*as literally as possible*! Really, it is the only *safe* way, keeping in mind that inevitable post-life meeting with God. If Jenna decides to start obeying the go-out-go-potty command in part only, we are going to have problems. If she decides to discard the "go potty," then she will not perform her responsibilities once we go out. If Jenna decides to remove the "go out" from the equation, suddenly she is squatting in the apartment, and I've made it clear how I feel about that. Our connection suffers if she cannot obey fully.

Yes, there are a number of ways to interpret complicated Bible passages and a number of solid denominations based on these variances. The point is not that one denomination is superior to another; the point is that the strength of the Christian organization is based on proper valuation of the book God gave us. When we, as churches or as individuals, adhere to the clear regulations of the Bible, our connection with God grows. When we start to remove or modify portions of the Bible to "fit the times," we are headed toward danger—formulating our own religion. God is eventually going to ask us about the parts we neglected.

We can adopt any belief system we want, but if it isn't God's system, then it isn't truth. If it is God's system, then we can expect to see responsibilities. But we can't let these responsibilities cloud the fact that there are benefits—that God likes to see us happy. God's system has the proper balance of responsibility and benefit. If we can't figure out the benefits, it would be wise of us to invest in the responsibility of reading his words in the Bible. Only as God's belief system becomes our own will we truly start to understand the depth of our responsibilities...and his benefits.

> Every word of God is pure: He is a shield unto them that put their trust in him. Add thou not unto his words, Lest he reprove thee, and thou be found a liar.
>
> Proverbs 30:5-6 (KJV)

God's Best Friend

Every now and then, my wife and I will take Jenna outside and run her until she is totally exhausted. We bring a tennis ball and a Frisbee, and Jenna's head just spins with excitement. I take the Frisbee and hide it behind my back, and my wife throws the tennis ball as far as she can. Jenna is instantly in hot pursuit. When she catches up with the ball and brings it back, I reveal the Frisbee. When Jenna sees it, her mouth drops open in amazement at her good fortune, and out comes the tennis ball. I throw the Frisbee, and Jenna chases, and my wife picks up the tennis ball for the next round. After about ten rounds of no-rest, non-stop fetching action, Jenna is panting and wheezing. We know we will have a nice quiet evening after we tire her out.

On one such occasion, we ran Jenna pretty hard, and after we had our fun, we came back inside. I noticed a slight hobble in Jenna's step but didn't think much of it. She crashed for the routine post-workout nap once we got indoors. But a little later, when she got up, she was limping badly on one of her front paws. It continued to get worse as the evening progressed, and in every step I could see the agony of her movement. I knew she was in a bad way because she was slow to come even when I held up a piece of food. Eventually she stopped walking altogether and just lay on the floor.

It was very painful to watch Jenna in this condition. My wife and I did everything we could for her. We tried to diagnose the problem, but it seemed to be an internal muscle injury, no cuts or abrasions to patch up. We tried to pinpoint and massage it for her, but that didn't do much. We babied her, giving her treats and food without making her move. We even prayed for her. We eventually decided to give it a little time, and if it wasn't better in the next day or two, we would take her to the vet.

The rest of the evening proceeded as normal, and eventually we went to bed. Jenna hobbled in painfully and lay down on her comforter on the floor, which is on my wife's side of the bed. Typical to our nightly routine, I read for about fifteen minutes after Danielle had turned out her light. When I finished reading, I got up to get a drink. On a standard night, Jenna watches me carefully when I come back to the bedroom. When she hears the creak of the bed as I sit down, she pops up out of her sleep spot and comes over for thirty seconds of goodnight petting. But that particular night, with her injury, I wondered if she would get up.

After I got my drink, I walked back to the bed, sat down, and looked over at Jenna. Despite her condition, despite her pain, she slowly got up and meandered weakly over to me, limping all the way. She fought through the nos her body was telling her to come over and give me my goodnight. I didn't have any food. I didn't entice her with a toy. She came over to see *me* and me alone. It was only my presence, my love, that she wanted. In that moment, I knew for certain that Jenna cared about me.

The Luxury of Love

Jenna obviously needs sleep and food to maintain her physical well being. Her physical needs are quite apparent; any dog owner knows they must feed their dog. Jenna also needs an element of fun in her life to maintain her mental balance, which the Frisbeeing often supplies. Her mental needs are less obvious than her physical ones, but the effects of neglect are real. Besides the physical and mental needs, Jenna has an even deeper need that she can barely grasp. Jenna needs love.

Love can be a controversial subject. Though love is a prevalent theme in stories throughout human history, and something we all experience in some form or another, little can be done to actually measure this substance. Because it is virtually immeasurable, we have a hard time comparing the love one person experiences with another person's definition. Furthermore, there is no conclusive evidence that humans or dogs *need* love to survive or thrive. Love is sometimes considered a luxury, not a necessity.

I'd like to think that our apartment is filled with love. But does Jenna need that love to survive? Perhaps not. If we released Jenna into the wild, her inability to forage for food would undoubtedly be her biggest problem. She would probably not worry about love too much when she was hungry. Starvation would be a much bigger threat at that point than lack of love. Her body does not immediately stop functioning because she feels unloved.

The dog, however, is probably the best-domesticated animal on the planet. This is how it got the classic nickname "man's best friend." There are ways it can survive physically without love, but there is a companionship tendency deep within the dog's genetic makeup. This tendency makes it prone to being an excellent friend to the human race. The dog can live its life entirely without the human touch, but I dare say that the best life a dog can hope for is under the care of a responsible, loving master. Jenna has the best life I can possibly afford to give her. For her, it sure beats knocking over trashcans looking for food.

Many psychological experts will tell you that a dog does not have the ability to love like a human. This may be true, but there are definitely trace elements of a substance we could call *love* coming from Jenna, as in the example of pressing through her leg injury. She got up and hobbled over to me because she wanted my affection. She wanted my love. She may never fall deeply in love with another dog like a human can with another human. She will never say the words *I love you*. But she can understand that I love her, and she can return the feeling to the best of her ability.

From my perspective as master, I don't care how advanced Jenna's ability to love is. Her quality lifestyle is afforded by *my ability to love her*. It isn't contingent on full reciprocation on her part. She is internally geared to be a companion to me. Her life is filled with love, though she might not even realize it. She might not recognize the food or the play as acts of my love for her. She may never see love on a human level, but it is definitely a part of her everyday life.

Can God love as deeply as a human? Obviously, yes; we've already seen how much he outranks us in basically everything. The real question becomes, can a human love as deeply as God? Just because our love can feel so real to us, we think we are experiencing "the real thing." But a life under the mastership of God is filled with love that we can't even fathom. It is filled with provision that we don't even associate with love. The whole system—the swats, the nos, the encouraging words, and more—is all built on the cornerstone of love, and we can barely even realize it. The best we can do is exhibit trace elements of the kind of love God shows us. It is intrinsic to desire this love.

There are some "tough cookies" out there who may claim that they don't need love. I will agree that the human body may not directly need love to function or stay alive, but we certainly have the option. Like a dog, there are certain things we are geared for—certain circumstances in which we flourish, whether we *need* them or not. We too have a companionship tendency that cannot be suppressed. And though we often substitute human companionship, there is a deeper companion with whom we are geared to associate.

Humans are geared to be the companions of God—"God's best friend," so to speak. We can *choose* to go without love and we can *choose* to go without God. But in making the choice to go without either of these benefits, we also are choosing a life of deficiency—a life that is only a fraction of how good it can be. There will always be an emptiness inside of us without these elements. We can never live the spiritually privileged life if we do not submit to God and his love for us—if we do not recognize his friendship.

Jenna had to battle her way to her feet that night, and she had to overcome a lot of hurt to get to me. Fortunately, it turned out that nothing was broken, and she just needed to rest her leg a few weeks. But that short walk across the bedroom was hard for her. And likewise, walking with God is not always going to be easy. Fighting through our struggles and our wrong desires can be challenging. But Jenna saw something more important than her struggle that night. She saw her relationship with her master and made it the most important thing in her mind. This relationship fueled her to get up and give me an illustration of the kind of determination we need to have. I was so proud, so flattered, that Jenna would go to that trouble for me. If we make our relationship with God more important than the work it may take to get closer to him, he will be pleased. He will undoubtedly unlock some extra affection for us.

God enjoys our obedience, and it builds up our relationship with him. But it means so much when he sees us actually *living* that relationship. When we choose God over our desires, even over our own comfort, he sees and honors it. Our relationship with our master strengthens when we put him above all else in our lives. And the measure of the strength of our relationship with God is often the measure of the blessings we will see. When we elevate God, he elevates us.

> ...there is a friend that sticketh closer than a brother.
>
> Proverbs 18:24 (KJV)

Part 5:

God and the Child: The Significance of Two-Way Communication (Prayer)

God the Father

God makes a great president. He acts as a wonderful boss. And he is a friend that sticks closer than any earthly brother. And that's it. That's the end—as much as we can ever learn about God. We've got him completely figured out…

Now, even if you can't pick up on my sarcasm above, the mere length of the remainder of this book should tell you that I wasn't being serious. It sometimes takes leaps and bounds just to get to the point of trusting God as more than a dictator, and we've covered a lot of ground so far. But if we believe that in our seventy or eighty years on this planet we can come to a full understanding of exactly who God is, we've got it all wrong. There is no end to his depth, especially from the perspective of a limited human. We can always continue to go farther.

So what is farther than friend? What is the next step? Well, instead of looking at just one biblical story or hero, let's take a glance at the span of biblical history. Let's see what God wants us to know about the history of his relationship with mankind.

In the Bible, the Old Testament focuses on one particular group, the Israelites, today known as the Jewish people. The Israelites were God's chosen people. He hung out with them and provided for them, and they transmitted his words, the developing Bible, from generation to generation. Over the duration of the Old Testament, the Israelite people often saw God as their president, a distant authority whom they feared. They saw him as their boss, especially when he brought commands and punishments their way. And a few Israelites, such as Moses and King David and Father Abraham (an ancestor to Israel), even viewed God as a friend.

Those who saw God as a friend had some amazing experiences. They overcame some amazing obstacles and challenges. They even had some amazing shortcomings. And although there are allusions and exceptions, the Israelites of the Old Testament didn't go much past the friend relationship with God. In fact, a great many of them reverted to seeing him only as a boss, and therefore they got hung up developing elaborate religious rules to obey. They forced these rules on others (much like we see today), and many people were turned off to the whole God thing. The entire nation of ancient Israel began to go down the tubes morality-wise as more and more of them turned away from having a relationship with God.

At the end of the Old Testament and leading up to the New, the Israelite people had been decimated by the surrounding enemies. Their nation and religion were in shambles, with little hope of recovery. Still, a select few were waiting and praying to God for a turnaround, much like I had been in my own life. Fortunately, God looks out for his friends.

In the New Testament, as the prayers for deliverance continued, Jesus stepped onto the scene. Most Americans have heard of this fine fellow. He introduced the Jewish people to a new way of thinking. Jesus talked about God all the time; the religious leaders couldn't get him to shut up. Jesus didn't usually refer to God as a boss. Sometimes Jesus referred to God as a friend. But most of the time, when Jesus spoke about God, he called him *Father*. For those ancient people, it was a revolutionary way of looking at God, which was often dubbed heretical.

My Dad's Love

Personally, I have a wonderful, loving father to look up to here on earth. My dad isn't perfect, as he'll admit, but he has always been there to help me understand that a relationship can go deeper than just friendship. He illustrates this in his willingness to help me anytime, anywhere. I sometimes hesitate to ask my friends for help; I don't want to be an inconvenience to them. But my dad will inconvenience himself greatly on account of me, and he will enjoy every minute of it. My dad wants to see me succeed so much that my success becomes his joy. As a result, he is willing to drive four hours to see me at the drop of a hat. If I need something from him, like help with moving or a big project, I just tell him the time and place, and he is there. We are more connected than just friends. In fact, to him, I outrank each and every one of his friends.

I understand that in this day and age, not everyone has such a paramount example of fatherhood in their lives—a relationship beyond friendship. This is unfortunate, of course, but it shouldn't hold us back. You see, I know that my dad loves me. But *love* is such a difficult word to define. How much does he love me? Where are the boundaries to his love, if any? We may comprehend the social meaning of *love*, but the only way to truly give definition to the word is to love someone for ourselves. Without practical application, *love* means only "really, really like."

I can be loved by a great many people and still never understand what love is. Contrarily, I can be hated by everyone and still somehow learn to love. Learning to love is not limited to certain social conditions. Each one of us has the opportunity to understand what love is, but no one is forced. Like the choice to believe in God, we have to make a choice to love others. If we do not, we cannot begin to comprehend the love of which God is capable. We won't even understand other people if we refuse to love. Without love, life makes a lot less sense. Without love, the desire to live begins to dwindle.

I might not be able to fully grasp the love that my dad has for me in large part because I am yet to experience fatherhood to the extent that he has. But I know that the love from my father is there, and I know I can give it back. In fact, I can give love out to whomever I please. I don't have to base it on anything—other people's abilities, looks, smarts, or qualifications. I can give love in "friend-like" helpings, or in "father-like" helpings. I don't even have to discriminate based on species. Love can bridge the gap between a human and a human, or a human and a dog, or a human and a cat, or a human and a guinea pig named Gizmo.

Our Dad's Love

What Jesus was saying when he called God our Father was that the relationship with God could go deeper than humankind had previously conceived. There is love out there that exists in quantities too great for humans to understand—a love that bridges all gaps. We are loved in a way we may never realize, much like I cannot yet fathom the love of my father for me. But we can give God our love back, and we can give it to others around us. Jesus himself said that the two greatest commandments were to love God and to love each other and not necessarily to follow some pious religious instructions (Matthew 22:36-40).

The Bible says, "Beloved, let us love one another: for love is of God; and everyone that loveth is born of God, and knoweth God. He that loveth not, knoweth not God; for God is love" (1 John 4:7-8, KJV). If we don't begin to give love out, we can't ever understand the fatherly love that God has for us.

I am now "Daddy" to Jenna. But it hasn't always been that way. Our relationship had to go through some stages before she would recognize me as more than a boss or a friend. Fortunately, Jenna blew through those stages. It took me at least a few visits to truly warm up to the pup, but Jenna gave me love from day one. She's got love, her doggy version of it, coming out her ears. The earlier stages of our relationship are prerequisites; she must obey me and befriend me. But the payoff is the love that fuels our connection to new heights. As I love Jenna more, she loves me more, and vice-versa. It's a wonderful cycle. Love is the substance that builds relationships beyond the acquaintance level.

Maybe you don't feel very loved, or perhaps not very lovable. Maybe you can't figure out why God would care about you. I know I've felt that way before, especially during the depressing times after my girlfriend left me. I was feeling so sorry for myself that I completely forgot about other people. I neglected connection—I forgot to practice love. Suddenly it felt like no one loved me anymore. I was surrounded by stifling loneliness.

But you know what? Through all my struggles, through my introversion and neglect, through my drugs and depression, my dad still loved me. One human cared about me *no matter what I went through*. In fact, I had a lot of family and friends who cared about me, but I was blinded by my own lack of love. I couldn't see others' love because none was coming out of me.

God cares about humans—those who are his children—in the same way that my dad cares about me. It doesn't matter if *I* can't see it; that love still exists. In fact, if I can't see it, it is my own fault and certainly not God's. Love holds faltering humanity together just like it holds Jenna and me together even after she takes a dump on the carpet. Without love, everything would fall apart. We need to practice loving each other if we want to understand the love that is God's glue for society. Once we refresh this understanding, we will realize that we are both lovable to God and loved by him.

An Impossible Love

God's love, the love that undergirds our society, is a constant. I realized that I could not get away from the love of either my heavenly Father or my earthly one, no matter what I did. But the next practical problem I faced was that the people around me were so darn tough to love. It didn't matter what circle I hung around with, churchies or non-churchies, there always seemed to be a heavy mix of the hard-to-love type. Even if I knew I had to love others in order to understand God, it still didn't make the task any easier. God is all powerful, so it must be easy for him to love the unlovable, I thought to myself. But how can I do the same?

Let's look back at how God expresses his love. One of the ways that he shows his care for us, as stated in earlier chapters, is through his provision (the first way *I* could understand). God provides an environment in which we can succeed, much like the US government (represented by the president) provides opportunity for the citizens. I see the results of this provision, afforded by both God and America, when I look at my job and my home and the food on my plate. Though I have a tendency to take these provisions for granted, they are nonetheless real-life illustrations of care for me.

I had some thoughts and theories about active love, but I was still having a tough time figuring out this love-and-provision connection. Fortunately, I had some help from the lady that was administering my drug-related probationary program at the time. No, she didn't sit down and have a deep theological heart to heart with me, and it probably wouldn't have worked if she had tried. She just assigned me the standard community service hours that went with my particular drug-offense package. I chose a soup kitchen.

People at the soup kitchen were not so fortunate to have many of the provisions that I had taken for granted. Specifically, the people that came to the soup kitchen needed food. They desperately needed someone to provide for them. And for those few hours on Saturdays, I got to be that someone. I got to help provide for their needs.

My first thought when I originally heard I would have community service was, *Oh, crap.* In fact, it was probably more profane than that. But the soup kitchen showed me the elementary principles of loving others. Love begins with provision—providing others with something they need. I didn't have to have a warm, gushy feeling in my heart when I *started* handing out dinner rolls and baked potatoes. I could begin with a chip on my shoulder if I wanted, and I usually did. But after I saw around a hundred people go through the line, destitute of food and dependent on me, thankful for every morsel, it changed me a little bit. The things that bothered me became a little less pervasive. The connection to the people I served became a little stronger. As I handed out roll after roll, I began to care for those people week after week. I began to actually *love* them—a crew of arguably unlovable characters. I began to understand love again.

It isn't a shame that so many needs exist; it is a shame that those needs are not provided for by those who can. Every need is an opportunity for love—to learn about love, to understand love, to get love, and to receive love. Just like faith does not activate if I sit on my duff, so too love does not have any use while lying dormant. If I ever want to understand levels of love as high as "unconditional love," I have to start with "beginner love." And beginner love is the ability to force yourself into service situations because you know the love that develops will be worth the cost of the service.

If you want to go farther with God, you've got to go farther with your fellow man. It doesn't matter what level of theologian you are; without love we cannot identify with the Father. Without love, life is being traveled in vain. Without love, we have no purpose. A world without love is a dismal place for man, woman, boy, girl, and even dog. But *with* love, life becomes worth living, and then it goes beyond.

> If I speak in the tongues of men and of angels, but have not love, I am only a resounding gong or a clanging cymbal. If I have the gift of prophecy and can fathom all mysteries and all knowledge, and if I have a faith that can move mountains, but have not love, I am nothing. If I give all I possess to the poor and surrender my body to the flames, but have not love, I gain nothing.
>
> 1 Corinthians 13:1-3 (NIV)

The Length of Longing

We've already discussed how amazingly genius you and I are…compared to a dog. I certainly know what Jenna needs, and I often know what she wants, typically before *she* even realizes it. But I do love to see her dog psychology at work. Even though I can read her like a book, I still enjoy watching her try to outsmart me or hide her true thoughts. Sometimes I pretend that I don't understand what she wants simply for the sake of entertainment. She gets all uppity, forgetting that I know more than her doggy brain could ever hold.

Jenna's potty breaks are pretty regular throughout the day, but on occasion my wife and I get busy and let Jenna wait a bit too long. If we aren't home, it's doggy poo in the living room, but if we are home, Jenna gives us fair warning. Her first step is eyeing up the leash. She stares at me until she gets my attention, then she looks at the leash. Then she looks back at me, then at the leash. Sometimes I egg her on with a classic, Lassie-style "What is it, girl?" She gets excited that I am listening to her but disappointed that I'm obviously not conforming to her desire.

Pretty soon, if I fail to respond by grabbing the leash, Jenna concludes that I must have no idea what she is asking for. So she moves on to stage two. Jenna's second step is the in-my-face approach. She comes up to me as close as I will allow and starts the panting. She stands there, eyes fixed on me, panting louder and louder. If I pretend to ignore her, she just keeps it up. If I *try* to ignore her, it doesn't work. Eventually, if I'm really resistant, she moves on to the final step—whining. When she gets to that point, I know I have about five minutes before I'll be cleaning the carpet. So of course I take her outside right away.

I know that Jenna needs to go out, but I still like to see her "ask." She does the same routine if she goes too long without food or water. These provisions are pretty much automatic in her life; I will provide them as long as she is my dog. I like the fact that she has come to recognize me as her provider, as her bugging me illustrates. It makes me feel like I am an important, recognized, and even beloved part in her life.

Most of us have thrown some desperation prayers at God, especially when we have an important or urgent need. When there's something going wrong in our lives, like Jenna's swelling bladder or empty stomach, we try to get God's attention with a prayer. We tell him our problems, and we hope he comes through. When it appears that he hasn't figured out what we need, we start to get concerned and get even more in his face, aggressively justifying our need. Finally, as we approach the verge of giving up, we start the whining and complaining. I know I've gone through the routine over and over again.

The purpose of talking to God is not to present a good argument or whine about what is going on. God already knows exactly what we need better than even we know. The purpose of talking to God is not to irritate him into submission—obviously we want to be cordial and respectful with him. The purpose of prayer is to establish a line of communication, letting God know that we see him as our caring provider and an important part of our lives. And if we pay attention to the *results* of our prayers, we will find that his love is true.

I love that Jenna comes to me with her problems. What I don't like to see is that she often forgets about me once her problems are solved. When I have a piece of cheese she wants, I'm suddenly Mr. Popular. Once I give her the cheese, I'm yesterday's news. I get very little thanks for my contributions to her life. She often forgets about my provision until the next need arises. I prefer that our communication is all day long.

So many times, I can be just as guilty as Jenna of taking provisions for granted. I see and feel the love of God in the way he takes care of me, yet I don't thank him enough. I seem to forget what he has done until the next hardship arrives. Often the only time God hears from us is when we need him, just like some people only call their parents when they need to be bailed out. This is no way to build a relationship. Love must be year-round, rain or shine. That's how freely our Father doles it out to us.

Years ago, I prayed a prayer for God to bail me out of my depression, drugs, and alcohol. I prayed it desperately, hopefully, and fearfully. I tried to get God's attention. I did a lot of huffing and puffing. I even did some whining and crying. And you know what? Over the course of time, slowly but surely, almost unnoticeably, *God gave me exactly what I asked for*. I didn't even realize his work in it—his constant provision—until I finally looked back over those years in retrospect. Then I could see what amazing things God had done for me. Then I could realize how thankful I should have been all along. I didn't pray a prayer and see the results the next day. I prayed a prayer and saw the provision of circumstances that eventually freed me from my addictions.

God likes to hear our requests, and he likes to hear our thanks. The Bible says, "Don't worry about anything; instead, pray about everything. Tell God what you need, and thank him for all he has done" (Philippians 4:6, NLT). There are many things to learn about prayer, but the most basic step is quite practical: do it, and do it regularly! God likes the sound of your voice. He likes to hear about the little things you think are trivial and the big things you think are impossible. He knows how communication, like community, is so important to humankind, and he wants to be a part of it—even though he knows exactly what we need and want.

Wandering Eyes

Jenna is a big fan of "dinner theater." When my wife and I sit down on the couch with a plateful of food, Jenna plops down on the front row for an event that is sure to be exciting. From there, Jenna carefully observes every morsel and movement of the ensuing meal. She watches each piece of food as it is transferred from the plate to our mouths, hoping for a fumble or a toss her way. It is obvious what she wants.

Once we finish the snack and set the plate down on the other end of the couch, Jenna returns her attention to us—or so it seems. But she just can't shake the thought of that food. There might be a few more crumbs on that plate, at least enough for a lick-full. She tries not to be too forward, but slowly she shifts her eyes oh-so-casually toward that plate. Then back to Mommy and Daddy, hoping we don't notice her secret desire. But we notice. And we laugh. In fact, oftentimes we put the plate in places she can see just to test her.

The bottom line is that she can't keep her inner thoughts from us. Her wandering eyes give her away every time. Humanity can identify. Our psychology is easily understandable to a superior being. Our needs are obvious to God. But we forget that we can't hide our desires any better. God sees our wandering eyes, and sometimes he smiles, and sometimes he frowns.

First the smiles: It is a frequent misconception that in the world of religion you must deny every human desire. Again, the stereotypical dedicated churchie is a straight-laced, no-fun-having wet blanket, here to make everyone miserable with his piety and self-denial. Now, the human condition is far from perfect, but there are good things about being a human. Some of the wants we have are legitimate, acceptable, and even condoned by our heavenly Father. We don't have to deny that we are a human, or that we have things we want out of this lifetime. Generally I don't mind when Jenna's wandering eyes spot a potential snack or her wandering nose smells a tempting treat. There's nothing wrong with a human wanting a good life, an attractive mate, financial stability, or a Snickers bar. In fact, if we don't want any of these things—if we aren't seeking to improve our lives somehow—then what is the point of pursuing God in the first place? Many of our human desires are excellent motivations for improvement.

Of course, there are desires that are not so healthy for us as well—the things God frowns about. We can't just do whatever we want and expect approval. He has addressed these unacceptable behaviors for the most part in the time-tested Bible he has entrusted to humanity. We've already discussed the route that consistent denial of God's principles will land us—in a world of hurt. I do have a problem with Jenna if her wandering eyes cause her to take *my* breakfast from me, like she did with Danielle's eggs. I also have a problem if Jenna's wandering eyes spot a ball out in the middle of the road or a porcupine on the loose. Ultimately, Jenna is the one that is going to have the problem if she pursues these things, and I just want to protect her. Likewise, God wants to keep us from having to be either punished or run over by a truck, which is why he frowns when we disobey.

Part of each of us wants the good things of God—who wouldn't? But part of us does not want to pay the price of subjection to him. Pursuit of God requires us to sort out our interior desires so that we can see what part of our human nature—our desire—is okay by his standards and what part is dangerous. Again, the Bible acts as a guide for what we should do and what we should not. And to enforce those desires that are acceptable, God has given us prayer. He wants us to speak to him about what we want so that we can not only identify him as our provider, but also so we can hear *his* intentions for us coming out of our very own mouths. The Bible compares the tongue, representing our speech, to the rudder of a ship. Such a small piece of equipment turns the entire ship, and so too the things that come out of our mouths set our courses through life (James 3:4-5).

God is listening to us all the time. He hears every word. He hears our requests, our complaints, and even our curses. When we direct some words toward him in prayer—preferably not the curse words—it not only shows him that we see him as a caring provider, but also that we recognize he is listening. Of course, he appreciates the recognition, but our prayers also help us to internalize the fact that God is up there and interested in our lives. Prayer is a win-win situation; God gets the glory he deserves as a caring Father, and we get the psychological provision we need to continue in a relationship with him. Prayer builds our relationship with God in many ways.

Unanswered Prayers

The big question, however, becomes, why doesn't God answer all my prayers? In other words, people may ask for a Lamborghini or a mansion or even the healing of a loved one and see no results. It doesn't seem like a caring Father would withhold anything good from his children, so why don't we get everything we ask for?

Well, there are two main reasons I don't give Jenna everything she "asks" for. The first reason is that what she's asking for may not be good for her. When Jenna sees something in my hand, she wants it. My animal-expert wife tells me that grapes are not good for a dog's system, but when I'm eating them, Jenna is begging for a couple. She doesn't even know what is good for her, but I do, so I avoid the doggy diarrhea and withhold this "good thing" from her. God does the same thing with us, as we've touched on before. Just because we want something does not make it a good or suitable thing for us to have. We may be asking amiss (James 4:3). God, by his nature, does not answer prayers for things that would ultimately harm us.

The second reason that I don't give Jenna what she wants is that the timing is wrong. As I've mentioned, I am ready and willing to provide Jenna everything she needs, and even for many of her wants. I delight in giving her the things she asks for that are truly beneficial to her. However, she is the dog and I am the master. If Jenna indicates with her panting and prodding that she wants to go out and play but I am in the middle of watching a TV show, she is going to have to wait. By position, my plans outrank hers—even something as meaningless as TV. It certainly doesn't mean I don't want to play with her or to give her any good thing she wants. It just means she is going to have to wait until her request fits into my plan.

God is the same way. We want things now, but he works on a little different time schedule than we do. By our subordinate position, we cannot expect for our whimsical plans to cancel out his long-term operation. Most of the time what Jenna perceives as a *no* is simply a *later*. God wants to give us the good things we want, but that doesn't mean whatever we want whenever we want it.

If we want good things from God, we need to work to understand him and his plan so that we do not ask for things that are unhealthy. We need to be patient as we realize that God is going to work within *his* timing. And we need to remember and cling to what we've asked for so that God can get appropriate credit—the thanks—when our answer comes about. Here again, verbalizing our prayers helps us to make a "hopeful thought" a little more tangible.

So if you meet the first checkbox (the thing you are asking for is something God wants you to have) and you meet the second checkbox (the thing you are asking for falls into God's plan and timing for you), do you get what you ask for? *Yes*! Think about it; if it is something God wants to give you and the timing is perfect by his standards, why wouldn't he give it to you? God is ready and willing to give you those good things that your heart desires—it is all part of his loving plan as our Father. Jesus himself says, "Therefore I tell you, whatever you ask for in prayer, believe that you have received it, and it will be yours" (Mark 11:24, NIV).

It almost sounds too good to be true—that we can have whatever we want from God. And in practical application, the theory also seems to have some flaws. Well, as I have found out every time I question God, the flaws are not on his side of the equation. He didn't put those words, "it will be yours," in the Bible to throw us off track. He wants to give us the good things, the benefits of a close-knit relationship with him. If anyone fails to make the cut, it is humanity, not God.

Jesus hits some important, semi-subtle keys to getting "whatever you ask" in this verse. There are some conditions. The first as that we must *believe.* We have to have faith in God, that he is benevolent and desiring to give us these good things. Most of us have at least a limited amount of this faith, as our pursuit of God evidences. But the second condition is that we must *receive.* If God gift-wraps exactly what we want and places it right in front of us, we must accept the gift or it does us no good. The only thing that ever slows God down is us—our lack of belief and our lack of receipt.

And here we come full circle. How do we increase our believing and our receiving? Through prayer! Through communication with God. What God wants to happen in our lives requires our cooperation. And cooperation requires communication. God speaks all sorts of languages and dialects—we've already discussed some of his techniques for getting our attention. The closer you get to God, the more you like what he says. The more sense it makes to you. The more he becomes like a Father to you. The more *blessed* your life becomes.

> You parents—if your children ask for a loaf of bread, do you give them a stone instead? Or if they ask for a fish, do you give them a snake? Of course not! If you sinful people know how to give good gifts to your children, how much more will your heavenly Father give good gifts to those that ask him.
>
> Matthew 7:9-11 (NLT)

> And don't worry about food—what to eat and drink. Don't worry whether God will provide it for you. These things dominate the thoughts of most people, but your Father already knows your needs. He will give you all you need from day to day if you make the Kingdom of God your primary concern.
>
> Luke 12:29-31 (NLT)

Triple Treats

As humans, we've got some pretty hard heads. I know I've proven it over and over again with my repetitive mistakes. We've already discussed three languages and dialects that God uses to try to get through to us. The first, of course, is pain, which is like a wake-up call in the simplest form we can interpret. Pain can show us that what we are doing should probably be examined to see if it lines up with God's program. The second language God uses is simply the *nos* and *thou shalt nots* that we hear in a lot of church sermons. These verbal negative reinforcements attempt to allow us to avoid the pain approach, if we will listen. Many people reject God and church because of the potential confinements and judgments on their lifestyles. Unfortunately, these people are in for some pain, but even worse, they may never see God for what he truly is—so much more than just a law giver.

God doesn't speak simply negatives and nos. He also has many *yeses*, which are found in the pages of the Bible. Yeses are the third method of communication. God has recommendations for behaviors that will not only keep us from pain and judgment, but will also direct us toward a positive life. He encourages us to live a "good" life—a life that is lined up with his plan. The initial benefits of this life are stability and optimism, but to believe that God stops there is again to underestimate him. He knows how to give provisions, but he also knows how to give above and beyond.

The fourth method of communication God uses to "speak" with man is *blessings*. A great many people never reach this level of the relationship with God, too turned off by rules or laws in their lives. But God can dole out positive reinforcement to his children as well. In fact, he prefers to. Whereas disobedience requires punishment, obedience is met with rewards.

So what are the rewards? Well, some people will go all spiritual on you and say things like "inner peace" or "a sense of deep contentment." These answers are all well and good, but a bit impractical, at least as the pursuit of God is in the early phases. When I was struggling with drugs and depression, these answers didn't even have applicable meaning to me—they were just nebulous terms like *God*. I really didn't even know such things truly existed. Granted, these internal rewards began to grow in their value as my pursuit developed (and they outweigh the physical), but let's start with the most physically applicable blessings before we deal with the intangibles.

Roll Over

Do you know what Jenna thinks is the best blessing on earth? Food. More specifically "treats." She knows that when she does something noteworthy, like peeing outside, she is sure to be rewarded with a treat. To her, treats make life worthwhile. For the sake of a treat, she will try her best to obey my commands. I have Jenna's undivided attention when I hold a treat in front of her nose.

To me, Jenna's treats mean very little. I could probably afford to go buy her a lifetime supply of treats with not too much strain to my wallet. They're only a couple bucks a bag. Treats are very easy for me to provide. Not only that, but they are hard and tasteless to me (I've tried them), so to a human they are of very little value. I have much better things to eat come dinnertime.

Yet these tasteless chunks mean the world to Jenna. Her eyes still bug out when I walk over to her treat container. At her level, it just doesn't get any better, and I enjoy her simplicity. I look forward to opportunities to give her treats; in fact, I create those opportunities myself.

"Roll over" is one such opportunity. My wife can take credit for teaching Jenna "sit" and "rest" and even "shake." The performance of these tricks on command yields for Jenna treats galore. But "roll over" is primarily my doing. I began to work with Jenna to try to teach her this standard dog trick years ago, toward the start of my relationship with Danielle. I was in for a long and spastic process (training Jenna, not dating Danielle).

I first told Jenna to sit. She obeyed. Next, I told her to rest, or lie down. It took her a minute, but she obeyed. I then told her, "Roll over." She looked up at me like I was a space alien. I then displayed the treat I had in my hand, and said, "Roll over." Now she looked at me like I was a space alien *with* a treat—I had her attention. Unfortunately, she had no clue whatsoever about what it was I wanted her to do. But I didn't give up.

First, I tried to manually roll her over. With a 105-pound dog, that was no small task. Jenna's focus was 110 percent on that treat in my hand, so she really did not want to be jostled. She was willing to do what she knew to try to get the treat and frequently stuck out her paw to "shake," hoping that was what I wanted. But it was not, and the standoff continued. Danielle got in on the effort, but again Jenna resisted what seemed to be a distracting attack from the rear in her quest for that treat. The closest Jenna would come was "rest." I eventually gave up for that night and gave her the treat for her effort, assuring her we would try again soon.

The next episode, I gave her a little demonstration. Treat in hand, I lay down on the floor and rolled over, telling her "roll over" the whole time. Now I was a space alien rolling around on the floor with a treat. Jenna's eyes stayed connected to the treat the whole time, but her comprehension remained quite disconnected.

Eventually, with a combination of repetition and my wife's assisting sneak attacks, we got Jenna to lie on her side. She was heavily rewarded for this amazing step—bunches of treats—and when I said "roll over" she now knew the first part of the equation. But we still weren't done. Jenna was not a big fan of flipping over on her back, so there was still some serious work ahead.

One day, Jenna was being particularly rambunctious, just bouncing off the walls. We thought maybe we could use her exuberance to our benefit in the roll-over training. I got out a treat, and she obeyed with enthusiasm. I said, "Sit," and she plopped down as fast as she could. "Rest," and she was on the ground. "Roll over," and she flopped to her side, with just enough momentum for me to push her over the rest of the way for her first assisted "roll over." And the audience erupted!

Danielle and I showered Jenna with affection and treat after treat for this monumental success. Jenna was a little freaked out by the flip, but she certainly enjoyed the rewards. And we kept working on her. Eventually, she knew that if she lay on the ground and flopped around enough, I would give her a treat once she performed an accidental roll. Her understanding of what "roll over" required increased until she now performs it with some degree of regularity. After months of training, "roll over" has become part of Jenna's trick arsenal—another opportunity for her to get a treat.

There are some things God wants from us, as laid out in the Bible he has provided. There are opportunities to get rewards of all varieties if we can learn to obey his commands. To us, these rewards are spectacular. The tangible side of God's rewards includes money and anything it can buy, friends of the truest sort, and success in our endeavors. The intangibles truly include such things as peace, joy, and happiness. And while these things may mean the world to us, they are quite easy for God to provide. He has no shortage of bankroll, despite the economy, and he has a long list of wealthy people on his friend list. God's resources, even from a practical standpoint, are unlimited.

So how do we get these rewards? We've already gone through a number of the general prerequisites: Accepting God as our ultimate superior (president), submitting to his leadership (boss), building a relationship as his friend, and seeing him as our loving Father. Certainly blessings line the way throughout each of these steps, but as we draw closer to him, we are more apt to understand exactly what he wants from us. We are better able to see the road that leads to the blessings we want. We increase our ability to live a blessed life as we notice more and more opportunities around us.

Jenna didn't always know what I wanted her to do when I said, "Roll over." In fact, many of my commands are wasted due to her lack of comprehension. But with a combination of my repetitive training and her desire for the treats, together we opened up a new avenue for her to be rewarded. I persistently worked with Jenna, and when she finally listened and understood, the treat jar became a little more accessible to her. And I love it—I have given her more treats for rolling over than for any other trick. I have shown off her rolling skills to all my friends and family, and I continue to reinforce the behavior with rewards of every variety. Over all, the whole rolling over experience has made both Jenna's life and my life a little better.

The continuing truth is that we will all have to do some work if this whole relationship with God is going to advance. We are going to have to figure out what God wants us to do—which behaviors are going to be rewarded. Here again, the Bible is an excellent source of helpful information from a loving Father. Where some people see commands, I am beginning to see *opportunities for blessing*. The points that turn people off toward God are starting to excite me because of the possibility for great reward. If I can find out exactly what God means by his commands, exactly what he wants from me, I am setting myself up for some serious treats.

So let's talk about the most obvious treat there is: money. Money is quite tangible and quite desirable. I know it is for me. Fortunately God is loaded. I just need to figure out the "trick" to getting some of

God's wealth to flow into my life. What does God want me to do so he can reward me in the very tangible area of finances?

Finances and God—it's a tough subject. People see giving to God as an obligation, and everybody gets a little squeamish in church when they start talking money. The most popular argument against giving in the offering is, "I don't see why God needs my money." Let me be crystal clear—*he doesn't!* God doesn't need our puny contributions any more than I *need* Jenna to roll over. I will get along just fine if she never rolls over again. But Jenna is the one that is missing out if she doesn't do the tricks I tell her to. In the same way, *we* are the ones that are missing out on blessings when we don't take the opportunity to give to God.

The Bible tells us in Malachi, "'Bring all the tithes [10 percent] into the storehouse so there will be enough food in my temple. If you do,' says the Lord Almighty, 'I will open the windows of heaven for you. I will pour out a blessing so great you won't have enough room to take it in! Try it! Let me prove it to you!'" (Malachi 3:10, NLT). God has given us instructions here as to what we are to contribute to his Kingdom, and it is a hefty 10 percent of our income. Other passages also enforce this frightening amount. I have a strange suspicion that just about now many readers want to put this book down.

Well, let me tell you that I am an accountant by trade. I'm not a pastor (yet), and I'm not a church employee, so I have no personal financial benefit if you give lots or little to your church. And when I look at that 10 percent through my accountant eyes, I see a whole lot of "negative"—money going out and no money coming in. I am very skeptical whenever anyone touches my finances. Yet the Bible makes it clear that giving to God is going to be rewarded. If I can beat back my logical nature enough to pull off the "trick" of giving 10 percent to God, the blessings will follow. It just doesn't make sense, yet I can't expect everything from God's perspective to make sense in my eyes. I want the blessings of God more than I want to cling to my faulty logic.

Giving away 10 percent of my income does not sound very practical, especially back when I was struggling to pay the bills. Again, my accountant brain does not look too kindly on this proposition. However, the thing about giving to God is that it is very *practical application*. Physically speaking, it is easy to accomplish. The doctrines and theology surrounding God can be daunting, an inexact science (to us) at best. It seems it is often unclear what move to make. But giving a specific dollar amount, high as it may seem, is a very tangible form of obedience (or disobedience)—a practical way to test faith. While I might not be able to decode the mysteries of the Bible, I certainly have the mental capacity to count out 10 percent of my income, and I have the physical ability to reach into my wallet and pull it out. The only component that may be missing is the faith to release that money to God.

The Giving Test

God started out as a theory to me, and it went well. My pursuit of him was rewarding and my relationship with him was deepening, though I was still having some reoccurring addiction problems. But I was always searching for a practical way for a layman like me to apply my growing faith. So I decided to try this tithing theory out. It wasn't easy—there were a lot of things I could have used that money for, my drug fines being one of them. But somehow I swung it, and I started giving to the church. The next day, I did not win the Michigan Lottery. My budget actually tightened up even more. This is where the test of faith started to kick in.

God was figuratively saying, "Give and keep giving." The question was, could I do it? Could I perform this "trick" and receive whatever God was holding in his hand? Could I trust that what God was going to give me was good? Could I trust that he would give it to me if I obeyed his words? During this time, I failed in a great many areas in my obedience, but the tithe was one area I remained relatively strong. I kept giving through the tough times, not because I was so awesomely religious but because I wanted to see what was behind invisible Door Number One. I wanted to see God's blessing in my life.

The only time God disappoints us is when our expectations are not right. And in this case, my expectations were right on. I stuck with the tithing, taking God's challenge to "Try it! Let me prove it to you!" And I found out what I already knew—God is not a liar. I had a decent job. I got a better job. Then I got an awesome job, traveling the country. Then I got married to Danielle, who I met at my job. She also had a very good job. Then I got promoted. I suppose I am just an average, middle-class American these days—financially nothing spectacular compared to the nation's median. Yet compared to where I was just five years ago, the income to my home has tripled. Some people may see coincidence, but I see obedience. I'm doing the trick God told me to do, and the blessing is working.

I say all this not to toot my own horn, by any means. I am just illustrating a principle for activating God's fourth communication technique—blessing—and it is a principle that has worked for me. Nobody has to give anything; we continue to live in a free country. But we can't expect faith to work without actions, and we can't expect faith-based blessings to work without faith-based activity on our part.

God's blessings are certainly not limited to finances. There are many ways we can obey God and receive treats for our effort, just like Jenna has a number of rewardable tricks in her arsenal. We can give our time and be rewarded. We can give of other resources and be rewarded. We can resist certain ungodly situations and be rewarded. As humans, we might not understand God completely, but he is certainly the best rewarder around. His treats always hit the spot.

As we grow closer to God, we need to start to realize that life is not simply a series of unfortunate events. Every event, even the seemingly bad ones, is an opportunity to be blessed. God is looking to give us good things, and he is disappointed when he has to withhold them due to our disobedience. Fortunately, the next opportunity to obey always comes around quickly. If we can trust that God *wants to* reward us, *can* reward us, and *will* reward us, we will begin to listen closer. We will begin to obey at a higher level—a level that is not always so comfortable for us.

Jenna got past the discomfort of rolling on her back, and I rewarded her handsomely with the treats that she wanted. I still do. I got past the discomfort of giving to God, and God rewarded me for my increased efforts to obey him. He still does. If we do not push past our comfort level, letting God know that his commands continue to outrank our feeble opinions, then we will not advance in our relationship with him. God is a loving Father, but if we can't see him as such, it certainly isn't his fault. If we are coming to God with our desires, verbalizing them, acting in obedience, and expecting a reward, then we have come to the right place.

> Give, and it will be given to you. They will pour into your lap a good measure—pressed down, shaken together, and running over. For by your standard of measure it will be measured to you in return.
>
> Luke 6:38 (NASB)

The God Box

I want God to be a part of my life. His involvement is the only way I can hope for the best possible outcome. Of course, involving him is much, much easier said than done. There always seems to be something holding me back from letting him bless me as much as he wants to bless me. It certainly isn't *his* ability hindering my progress, so that only leaves one possibility—it must be my ability that slows him down.

Human beings, men especially, I'm told, have a tendency to compartmentalize everything. We take what we learn about dogs, for instance, and put it all into a little box in our brains. Then when a dog question arises, we open our "dog box" and let the information out. The compartments in our brains store all sorts of information about every topic and experience we've ever encountered. Some of the information is good and some is bad. Some is true and some is false. Occasionally the true and false boxes duke it out in our reasoning and consolidate to form what we conclude to be the most accurate information available on the given topic. We throw out or modify faulty data, and we keep and upgrade the good information. Through this process, we gain mental maturity. We break down the things that hold us back.

When I began to understand how my brain handles information, I also began to encourage this maturity process. Like any normal human being, I wanted the falsities and other garbage in my mind banished. I wanted to know the truth. Unfortunately, I was personally responsible for most of the trash I had accumulated. I had let society shape me, and society doesn't always know the truth. But there is someone who does have the truth, which is why I eventually turned to God as my primary source.

Like any other topic in my brain, I initially locked God away in a compartment. When I wanted to talk religion with my friends, out came the "God box," which my church-going parents had loaded throughout my youth. When the religious conversations were over, I put God back into his compartment and moved on to other items. I liked the setup; it was rather convenient for me. It fit into my mediocre-and-slipping life quite nicely. But God, as a loving Father, does not want me or any of his children to have a mediocre life. Remember, he has all those blessings lined up just for you. God wants to occupy more space in my life than just a little box because when he is left in charge of any area, it flourishes. God wants to be the *big* box—the *main* box—in my life, just like any good father wants to be involved in his child's thought process.

As my pursuit of God strengthened, the God box started to become sort of a rabble-rouser in my persona. As I said, I wanted the truth, which meant some of the compartments containing falsity had to be renovated or removed. Well, along those lines, the God box took some initiative on its own. It started to challenge the contents of some of the other compartments. I would open other compartments and find many of my previous belief systems seriously shaken up from an apparent tangle with the God box.

For example, thanks to the God box, I had to redefine the word *fun*. I had grown to believe that *fun* meant "reckless, selfish partying until you pass out." The God box said otherwise. The God box told me that this was not the true, God-intended meaning for the word. I liked my definition, but it was not the truth. Fun was not intended to destroy me, but "reckless, selfish partying" certainly could. So I had to renovate my fun compartment to comply with God's truth. It was a very difficult process, but the payoff is the more blessed life that I now live. The God box has already turned a number of my previous beliefs upside-down, and it continues to do the same today. The closer I get to God, the more I welcome the painful-but-beneficial mental maturing process that he inspires.

So these days, I enjoy the work of God on my mind. I try to keep my God box loaded and growing through church, Bible reading, and prayer. I want him to take on the untruths that still infect some of my mental compartments. I want to be as mature, as filled with the truth, as I possibly can be. And God wants the same for me as well. That's why he wants to make sure *every* compartment is subject to the truth. I still have a long way to go.

I do have a compartment that I unintentionally tend to keep separate from God. In fact, I would say that many of us face the exact same struggle. At one end of my brain is the God box, fueling a general sense of goodness within me. We tend to see the God box in sharp contradiction with perhaps the "evil box," which is loaded with such blatant negatives as hateful, hurtful, and even murderous desires. And certainly God is opposed to these things, hoping to banish them. But a great many of us have separated for ourselves a compartment that seems totally harmless and even appropriate. We have moved this compartment as far away from God as possible because the ideas inside either box can often seem so contradictory to each other. It is from this box that we pull much of our mentality, inadvertently neglecting what God has to say about these seemingly non-religious topics. This quiet yet powerful compartment is the "logic box."

Now let me start with a huge disclaimer right here and now: *I don't encourage anyone to throw logic out the window*. Logic has wonderful uses and is required on a daily basis. Much of this book is rooted in the logical thought process (though I suppose an ardent atheist may disagree). Those followers of God who entirely pitch their logic often give believers a black eye with their instability and ranting. Following our heavenly Father does not require that logic be abolished. In fact, God and logic go hand in hand. Let me qualify that statement: God and *God's logic* go hand in hand. God and *man's logic* is where the conflict begins in my mind. Man's logic—my "logic box"—does not need to be removed, but it constantly needs to be renovated. It constantly needs to be checked against the God box to make sure it lines up with God's truth. Any time our logic and God's logic conflict, we need to make sure it is God's logic that wins out.

Society, however, places immense value on man's logic. Herein lies one of our greatest problems. While we are a nation known for its worship of God, we also have promoted logic to higher and higher levels of prominence. I think we can accept that our personal logic is occasionally faulty, but when general social logic has reached a certain acceptance level we seem to esteem it as 100 percent truth. In this way, we let democracy decide truth for us. And we've titled our highest logic—the logic that contends with God's existence altogether—as "science." In a general sense, God and science (*man's* science) do not get along.

Again, I am not here to condemn science or logic. I simply want to show how science can be reconciled with a true belief in God. Most science can happily coexist with God. For instance, God and gravitational pull are in perfect harmony. Gravitational pull and God can both be entirely true—neither conflicts with the other. In fact, gravitational pull is a proven part of our ability to exist on earth and for the planets to stay in alignment. God does not conflict with nor refute gravity. Where we get into trouble is when we take things that are not proven—scientific *theory*—and promote it to *truth*. Science is not the villain *until we esteem it higher than the source of truth*. Anything elevated to this level is a danger to an appropriate relationship with the Father and a hindrance to a fully blessed life. The apparent conflict between God and science is because we are talking about *man's* scientific *theory*. The best we can come up with is not always right.

When two sources in one mind share a conflicting view of the same thing, one source must be right and one wrong. It is much like differing religions; if they have opposing views of God, they cannot both be right. Well, scientific theory, hereafter "science," sometimes conflicts with the Bible in its view of God. Science is quick to point out that there is no solid evidence for the existence of God. Of course, there is no solid evidence *against* the existence of God either. Much of the evidence that is out there, as "unsolid" as it may be, is subjective. That means it is subject to the person observing the evidence. One person sees a chance-driven close call—say, with a roll-over accident—while another person sees God's protection in his life. It can be interpreted either way, but a decision must be made at the *personal* level. This illustrates how God wants to involve himself in our lives through a personal relationship, not scientific proof. However, man's choice to believe does not necessarily offer scientific evidence of God's existence. Every person decides for himself how he will view his personal evidence; a person *must* decide, or he will spend his life conflicted and immature. Science will not bail us out on making a personal decision about God.

Let's say that, like me, you believe in God but see some serious conflicts between God and the science you have been taught—the God box and the logic box within your mind. In fact, let's cut right to the chase: man's origin. How did we get here?

Well, if you believe in God, you've already done the scientifically hard part. Science backs randomness as the source of human origin: a big bang or some other random occurrence as the beginning, evolution to develop life on the only supporting planet we know of, and chance as responsible for any other events that brought man into the picture. If randomness truly is the source of our existence, and God exists, then he must have stumbled onto the scene sometime after we originated. In other words, God was out perusing the universe, and he noticed earth beginning to thrive, and he said, "I think I'll be the God of that planet." Of course, this conflicts directly with God's all-knowing attribute—now we're talking about a god who is limited in his ability instead of the true God of the universe.

But if God is all knowing, he didn't scoop his knowledge up from the Internet—he knew it from the start. That means he was around from the origin of man, and, in fact, before it. His intelligence certainly qualifies him as able to engineer our measly (to him) universe. And if he is all powerful, he certainly has the ability to create it. So what does a logical being do when left alone in a field of space with infinite resources? The same thing I did when I was four years old and had a bunch of Lego blocks. He creates! God has the wisdom and ability to make the universe, so why wouldn't he?

The book of Genesis, the first book of the Bible, opens with the words, "In the beginning, God created the heaven and the earth" (KJV). This statement is just as true as the rest of the Bible. The passage goes on to explain some specifics of this creation process. The Bible's explanation has been viewed both literally and figuratively, but the most important part is "God created." A random origin for man, which may be housed in the "logic box," does not make logical sense next to a belief in God. Belief that God exists goes hand in hand with belief in him as our Creator.

I've often wondered why God loves us. We're rebellious, unbelieving, and failing miserably much of the time. But if God created us—if he is in essence our *literal* Father—it goes *part* of the way to explaining why he would care about us. He wants us to have a relationship with him, a relationship that outranks even our best scientific deductions. In fact, *he made us for this purpose.*

Now you may notice something missing from this chapter to this point: an illustration that compares the Jenna-and-me relationship with God and man. Perhaps this is a good place to point out that there are differences. I am not Jenna's god, despite the great number of relative relational similarities. Even though I act as her father and provider, I still do not possess the ability to create a "Jenna." Science may be able to manipulate and alter life in some ways, but our most brilliant minds still cannot create life from scratch. Life, the primary component of our existence, continues to be a mystery to us. Here, our ignorance again highlights our inferiority compared to the wisdom of God.

As the relationship with God progresses, we cannot forget his superior knowledge. As Jenna and I grow closer, she discovers things about me, and I discover things about her. But it is not so with God. He does not have to discover anything about us; he already knows it all. That means that if there are any deficiencies in the relationship, they are never God's fault. If I am distant from God, the culprit is obviously me. God is always playing his part. The relationship only develops if we play ours.

This places a large burden on the human end of the God-and-man relationship. Since God has no need for mental development, *our* understanding is the only variable in the equation. It took me so long to see God as a loving Father, but that doesn't mean he wasn't looking at me with the same love before I realized it. God doesn't become what we figure out; we figure out what he's always been. As we pursue him, we begin to see how wise he really is. Sometimes we tend to take a roundabout way to understanding what we have always been to God. As long as our understanding is growing, so can our relationship.

God behaves as our Father because he is our Father (who art in heaven). We are his children, and we have the responsibility to develop and mature. In a general sense, this is God's purpose for our lives. He wants us to grow in faith to a point that nothing can shake our trust in our heavenly Father. Nothing can outrank him. We need to put our logic and our scientific theory in their rightful place: under God. Sure, it takes faith to demote these highly esteemed contenders, but faith in God always brings rewards. And the more rewards we receive, the more our faith in our loving Father grows.

Through this faith-based cycle, we learn more and more about who God truly is.

> By faith we understand that the entire universe was formed at God's command, that what we now see did not come from anything that can be seen.
>
> Hebrews 11:3 (NLT)

> For I am the Lord, I change not.
>
> Malachi 3:6 (KJV)

Unleashed

As we discover more about God, we discover more about his role in the God-and-man relationship. As we understand his role in our lives, we begin to understand *our* role better. If he is the superior, that makes us the subordinates. If he is the Father, that makes us the children. And if we are his children, that means he has a purpose for us—progress he wants us to make. He wants to see our faith reach new levels so we can live more fulfilling lives.

Jesus lived a pretty important life on this planet (understatement). Historically speaking, he is *the* reason Christianity flourished and became a dominant world religion. He was sent directly from God the Father. Jesus's role in history was pivotal—defining, even—therefore, he had some pretty important responsibilities while a human. He had a purpose of utmost importance, and he and his followers knew it. But his followers didn't always get everything right.

One day a few local parents decided that they would like Jesus to bless their children. Sounds like a reasonable enough request to have this revolutionary teacher say a prayer for your child. So these parents brought the children to Jesus, but Jesus's followers stopped them in the path. The Apostle Peter was probably working the perimeter. Because Jesus had such important responsibilities—such noble purpose—Jesus's followers assumed that he did not want to be disturbed by something as trivial as children. But they assumed wrong.

When Jesus caught wind of the situation, he corrected his followers' error. He said, "Let the children come to me. Don't stop them! For the Kingdom of Heaven belongs to such as these" (Matthew 19:13, NLT). Jesus then blessed the children, as the parents requested. At another time, he told his followers, "I assure you, unless you turn from your sins and become as little children, you will never get into the Kingdom of Heaven" (Matthew 18:3, NLT). Jesus saw something important when he looked at the children. In fact, he indicated that what he saw in these youngsters was *essential* to following God. What was it?

Well, as you know by now, I'm big on *practical.* I appreciate the clear-cut, regulatable positives in my life: church attendance, Bible reading, prayer time, and even financial contributions. I know that obedience in these areas sets me up for blessings and success in my pursuit of God, and I can force myself to schedule or budget them even if I don't want to. But when I think about children, I don't think about rigid schedules. I don't think about regulations. The things I think about are much less tangible than that. When I think about children, I think about happiness. I think about joy. I think about magic.

There is something magical about children, something we adults sometimes can't put a finger on. Recently, my wife and I were stationed at the doors of our church to hand out some missionary information as the people walked in. Danielle gave a little boy, who was perhaps three years old, a simple Bible booklet about the size of a dollar bill. He lit up the foyer with his smile! We probably handed out hundreds of these standard-type booklets, many to indifferent adults, but this child's reaction takes the cake. No one could look at that little boy and his five-cent booklet and not smile—and not feel a little bit of joy bubbling on the inside. This boy's joy could not be scheduled. It could not be regulated. It wasn't even practical; *everyone* got a booklet. Yet this reaction made my morning better.

God loves to bless us with provision, finances, friends, and so much more. He enjoys seeing our success in these areas. But when

Jesus talks about the essential elements of following the Father—entering the kingdom of heaven—he is making sure we understand that there is more than physical success. Despite my appreciation for the tangibles, there are intangible attributes that must be considered in a walk with the Lord. God wants me to develop on the outside, no doubt, but he is much more concerned with the inside.

On the outside, a child might not have much. On the inside, however, most children are abounding with riches. They are humble, not thinking they are God's gifts to the earth. They are submissive to correction and authority, as we should be toward God. They are easy going, not prone to hurtful anger or holding grudges. And most of all, they have a faith that cannot be shaken. Tell a child about a loving God, and he believes whole heartedly, just like we adults should.

The faith of a child is an amazing thing, and it is an essential thing. I am very quick to consult the logic in my mind, but I am not always quick to *just believe*. But since God's logic is higher than mine, I'm not going to understand it some of the time. I'm just going to have to trust God—a being I can't see, hear, or touch (under normal circumstances). Trusting like this can be amazingly difficult… when you're an adult. But when you're a child, this level of belief is a piece of cake.

God's intent may be to prosper us physically, but more than that he wants to see our faith advance. He wants to take us from doubting adult to believing child, and this lifetime is his proving ground. At a low level of faith, it may take heavy doses of instruction, correction, and suggestion to get us on track, which is why I recommend accumulating the discipline required for regular church attendance. It sure helped me, and it continues to do so. As faith grows and our beliefs become more immune to doubt, some rigidity of regulation can be lightened. Church is always a good thing (the *right* church), but God wants our faith to be in *him* and not dependent on a building or schedule. He wants us to develop a faith that cannot be taken away—the faith of a child.

Unwavering Obedience

I talked about Jenna's leash in an earlier chapter. Jenna's leash, though confining, keeps her out of trouble and safely by my side. At her low level of obedience, the leash is a must. She believes I can protect and watch out for her, but sometimes she thinks that another dog across the apartment complex is more important than my protection. When she starts her naughty beeline toward the other dog, the leash keeps her from getting far. At her level of development, which is not likely to advance much further, she needs the leash to keep her connected to me. The leash, though it yanks on her neck, continually reminds her that I am by her side—her loving Daddy.

But there is a better way. Jenna is safe on the leash, but she is also restricted. If she could only trust that my judgment is superior, that flying across the yard at that other dog is *not* a prudent move, she would not need to be leashed all the time. If Jenna could develop her doggy belief to a point that says, "Daddy *always* watches out for me and knows what's best," then I could throw the leash out the window. She would stick by my side no matter what the situation—no matter what temptation came her way. Her faith in me would keep her on the straight and narrow, walking in safety and blessings for the rest of her life.

Jenna is a little more reckless than that, so I suspect she will forever need the leash (probably even in heaven). But I know that a high level of trust in a master is possible. I have seen dogs, mainly on TV, that *always* obey their masters' commands. They don't need a leash at all. Usually they are hunting dogs, trained to scare up or retrieve birds. These dogs display a level of obedience that is rare in the general canine populace. The master says stop and they stop. The master says go and they go. These dogs obey right and left commands, and some even obey speed commands (such as "slow" or "fast"). These dogs stay 100 percent in the realm of exactly what their masters want from them, no matter what distraction may be on the right or the left. I think Jenna operates at about 15 percent.

The point is that we have to learn to trust God more than simply on tangible terms. This can be a stretch for a "logical" person like myself. Church, the Bible, and all the commands of God can certainly act as a tangible leash, constantly requiring that I stay within certain boundaries laid out by the master. Yet even with this leash, I can be internally fighting to get away or to get a few more inches out of God. But if I can develop an internal level of trust—faith—in a loving Father, then getting away from him does not sound like such a good idea. As my faith grows, I *want* to stay beside him in the place I know is safe. The distractions around me don't look so good anymore when I realize that being at God's side is the best place I can be. When I reach this point, which may take excessive training, then the confinement of the leash is discarded. I have every human right to leave God—as do you—but I just don't want to anymore.

Do you know what those super-obedient hunting dogs get for their obedience? The answer is quite simple: Whatever the master wants to give them. Not only do they trust that their masters' commands are irrefutable, but they also trust that the reward for their actions will be appropriate. These dogs believe that what they get from the master will be better than anything they could provide for themselves. Granted, we do not always get exactly what we want from God, but we have to trust that his rewards are the best. The blessings of God come from a loving heart that hopes to see his children succeed. He wants us to be able to walk beside him without a leash, and he is patient in our training. But he also has an endless supply of good things to pour out upon us if we can make him the center of our efforts. As we advance our faith in God, he advances us in both tangible and intangible ways.

As I said, Jenna is probably somewhere around the 15 percent obedience level, and I love her just the same. We might have low levels of faith, but our loving Father still cares for us. His love doesn't stop, but he cares too much to see us live in mediocrity. He wants to see our faith increase. He dreams of a leashless walk for us loaded with blessings only he can provide within the safety of obedience. But we have to accept our role as children in his kingdom. We have to develop our relationship with him by trusting that his way is the best. We have to change on the inside.

God is an awesome Father. Believe it, and your life will continue to change for the better.

> The law of the Lord is perfect, reviving the soul.
> The decrees of the Lord are trustworthy, making wise the simple.
> The commandments of the Lord are right, bringing joy to the heart.
> The commands of the Lord are clear, giving insight to life.
> Reverence for the Lord is pure, lasting forever.
> The laws of the Lord are true; each one is fair.
> They are more desirable than gold, even the finest gold.
> They are sweeter than honey, even honey dripping from the comb.
> They are a warning to those who hear them; there is great reward for those who obey them.
>
> Psalm 19:7-11 (NLT)

Creature from Beyond

God cares about us; he wouldn't stick around if he didn't. He wants to build connections with us individually because he involves himself in our lives. He even wants to see us succeed and live lives filled with his blessings. So it would seem that, in theory, as soon as we accept him as our superior, friend, and Father, our lives would be a non-stop cavalcade of good things and happy times. Yet it doesn't work out that way.

We look around our world today, and we see some pretty disheartening happenings. In the big scheme, we see natural disasters, wars, and diseases, among other horrors. Shrinking the scope a little, we see community and family struck by accidents, sickness, and financial burden. Shrinking it even more, we see our own problems and struggles, which often appear insurmountable. The bottom line is that life is filled with suffering—globally, locally, and personally. How do all these agonizing hardships reconcile with a caring and just God? In other words, *where are all those theoretical blessings?*

These questions, and others like them, are what keep many people distanced from God for their entire lives. And don't get me wrong, they are good questions and must be considered in the advancement of a relationship with the Father. Bad things happen to good people all the time—it cannot be denied. In fact, even those people who seem to be upright, God-fearing believers encounter their "fair" share of tragedy. There doesn't seem to be any guarantees for anyone, believer or not. So what's the point of believing? Why cultivate a relationship with the Father if any one of us could be snuffed out at any moment?

I remember when I was very young, probably six years old or so, my family had kind of a scraggly-looking English setter named Creature. He was an outdoor dog. Being a kid, I was a little bit afraid of Creature, and I didn't venture too close to him without my dad beside me. Yet I somehow developed a mild connection with the animal and looked forward to seeing his familiar face.

On one occasion, as my family and I were returning home, we decided to check on good ol' Creature. We kept him on a chain connected to a fence near our garden, and we expected to see him romping around just like we had left him. We were in for a serious disappointment that day.

Creature had done something out of the ordinary while we were away. He had somehow managed to get his chain all twisted up on the fence. In his struggle to free himself, Creature had looped the chain around his neck and become tightly bound to the fence, seriously constricting his airway. Poor Creature was left without the oxygen he needed to survive. I'm sure he struggled valiantly, but by the time we got to him, there was no life left in his body.

I know he was "just a dog," and not one I was particularly fond of, but I cried my little eyes out. Death had never been so personal to me. This entirely innocent animal had his life stolen away from him. My dad and I took him into the woods and buried him, and I knew I would never see Creature again. He was gone forever. It just wasn't fair.

As a child, this was the first death that I really remember, but it was far from the last. I eventually saw grandparents and great-grandparents die. I saw friends and acquaintances pass. Some deaths seemed relatively fair, after a long and prosperous life. Other deaths were ahead of their time and left me with a sick feeling in my gut. The untimely deaths, which we've all seen, do not feel very fair at all. If God loves us, how could he let these bad things happen? Tough question.

Not Fair!

Let's first look at "unfairness" and figure out exactly what it is. I had loved Creature, at least a little, as evidenced by my sadness at his death. When Creature died, that was the end of him. Creature no longer existed. Yet my love for Creature was not so quick to perish. Death had taken him away, but it could not take away the feelings I had for him. My love for Creature outlasted his existence on this planet. And that is why I thought his death was unfair. Something in the physical realm was taken away while something in the emotional realm still remained embedded inside me.

This is the composition of most occurrences we dub unfair. There is a death—a separation—and something is taken away. A loved one dies, and he or she is gone. An accident happens or a disease develops, and health is gone. A financial crisis strikes, and money is gone. Something good always disappears. At the same time, something always lingers internally, be it a love for the deceased, a desire for a healthy body, or a craving for monetary security. Things go from "the way they were" to "the way they are now," and we want "the way they were" back. Sometimes people live their entire existences simply wishing they could have their glory days back, à la Al Bundy. When there is a disconnect between the way things are and the way we want them, the typical reaction is to claim unfairness.

Well, things in life are usually not exactly the way we want them, as we've already discussed. There is always an opportunity to say, "This isn't fair." Things were definitely not how I wanted them when Creature died—not very fair. Sure, I learned a lesson about life and death, but the cost was more than I personally wanted to pay. Undoubtedly, God could have stopped this death, but he did not. How could a father let his child go through this saddening experience?

Maybe my question begins a bit too theologically. What happened to poor Creature was simply scientific. In his stupidity, Creature had somehow wrapped his chain around his own neck. As it tightened, the result was simple: he strangled himself. Case closed. There is a biological law in place that says a dog cannot live without oxygen, and so when Creature inadvertently tried to violate this rule, his fate was sealed. It is the same fate every dog that chokes itself will get—an entirely fair result of attempting to break unbreakable rules.

Nobody seems to question natural laws. No one says that it isn't fair that we need food or water or oxygen to survive. Anyone who wants to protest these essential elements is welcome to. But living outside of these natural laws will most certainly yield death. If you break the rules and decide that you only want to breathe carbon dioxide, your end will be your own fault, a fair conclusion to foolishness.

Our Father obviously put these natural laws into place. Thankfully, they create an environment in which life can be sustained. Can we blame God and call it unfair if *we* decide to break theses rules? Hardly. But God put more than just physical rules into place—he put moral and spiritual rules in place as well. While obedience to the physical laws keeps us safe from physical harm, obedience to the moral and spiritual laws keeps our internal being alive and developing. When we obey the rules we see in the Bible or hear at church, we grow closer to God, which is spiritually the best place to be. Spiritual survival depends on obeying God's spiritual laws, just like physical survival depends on obeying his natural laws.

The consequences of violating natural laws are obvious: If you jump off a ten-story building, you *will* hit the ground. Unfortunately, ignorance is no defense once gravity kicks in. You may have a few seconds before impact to debate fairness, but in the end you cannot stop the result, and you will be held fully responsible for your decision to jump.

But what of the moral and spiritual laws that God put into place? Violation of these laws *seems* much less fatal than violating the physical laws. When we make a morally violating decision, such as stealing someone's car, we do not die instantly. We may have days, months, years, or decades to personally justify our actions and argue about fairness. But the eventual consequence of violating moral and spiritual laws is unavoidable, just like gravity. If God is to be entirely fair, we all must pay for every one of our moral and spiritual failures. Stealing carries a penalty, as does any one of the deviant behaviors described in the Bible. I don't decide what the penalty is, nor does the judicial system, necessarily. God has already decided on the consequence of stealing, just like he's decided on the consequence of jumping off a building.

When we see an "end" in our lives—an end of life or health or prosperity—it is always a consequence. For every effect, there is a cause. There is evil in our society, and there is evil that touches each and every one of us. We all do the wrong thing some of the time. Granted, the bad things we experience are not always a direct result of our own actions, but a result of a humanity that has been screwing up since the dawn of creation. The only consolation is that God is still in control. He can intervene any time the consequences of our fallen world start to play out.

Ultimate Unfairness

One of the greatest examples of unfair treatment is the life of Jesus Christ. This man walked the earth doing nothing but good—helping, healing, and teaching. Yet he did not receive a throne of honor among the people. Instead, the leaders despised him because he took the spotlight off them. It didn't matter what good thing he did; they saw it through morally clouded human eyes. They subconsciously decided to take out humanity's shortcomings on him, a man who had done nothing wrong. They brutally murdered this innocent man by nailing him up on a cross for the world to see. And as he was dying, Jesus sure could have presented an excellent case against fairness. Instead, he prayed that God would forgive these evil leaders. He knew he was about to die, and he also knew that under the control of God, justice is always served eventually.

Jesus understood that God's love for humanity exceeds an individual lifespan, much like my love for Creature exceeded his. Long before I was born, God was here. And you know, on the day I die, God will still be around. There is something very temporary about a human lifetime. I can be self-centered sometimes, and I forget about the fact that I am one of billions of people who will live and die on planet earth. One day I will be just a memory. Natural, moral, and spiritual laws will live on while I lay in my casket. These laws are certainly more important than I will ever be. They were designed to span the life of the earth no matter how pointless or unfair they may look to human eyes.

My problem is that I see unfairness from a human perspective. I see the death, and I feel the pain. I see emotion-violating tragedy, and I think it is not fair. I see "behind the times" moral rules and regulations, and I think they need human updating. I see spiritual truths and think they are spiritual "options." But God sees things from an eternal point of view. That means that to God, part of me lives on even after my human body cannot. To God, the moral rules he set up in the beginning will have the best possible results throughout the course of human history. He set them up for a reason. God holds the everlasting spiritual truths about life and death.

Unlike man, God's justice scale is eternity. The things we see as unfair are actually fair on a scale we do not yet understand. This is where our faith kicks in—faith that justice will *always* be served on an eternal scale. This is the faith that Jesus had as he walked the earth. Some people face death and as a result get farther from God. God's people face death and get closer to him. They understand that God is in control, and everything is eventually going to work out in this life or the next. For God's children, all things work together to bless them on an eternal scale.

> And we know that God causes all things to work together for good to those who love God, to those that are called according to His purpose.
>
> Romans 8:28 (NASB)

Part 6:

God and the Complete Human, Birth through Death: The Salvation Plan

God the Savior

God is our loving Father and all-knowing Creator. He set things up on earth just the way he wanted them to be. The natural laws he put in place are obvious boundaries within which we must live. The moral and spiritual laws are less obvious to our tainted perceptions, but God has given us ways to understand them. The consequence for excessively violating natural laws is typically death. The consequence for breaking moral laws is also the end of something, be it life, or freedom, or health, or innocence. But the spiritual laws—the realm of faith—are most important to God, because without faith, a person can't even believe in God or his rewards (Hebrews 11:6). Living a life entirely within the natural laws and even the moral laws is not enough to please God because faith is an essential element of God's spiritual laws. Fittingly, violation of spiritual laws carries eternal consequences.

So what are the consequences of violating a spiritual law? Just like natural and moral violations always create death of some sort, spiritual violations also have a destructive effect. This effect can be felt in the most precious commodity we have—our relationship with the Father. It is so important to God that we stay connected to him, but when we fail spiritually, we devastate the relationship. We've all violated God's rules in a way that could separate us from him for potentially a *very* long time.

You see, God operates on an eternal scale when administering spiritual truths. That means he is *forever* loving and *forever* just, to an extent humans cannot attain. In fact, God is himself *perfectly* good—naturally, morally, and spiritually. He has no evil within his personality, or else he could not be infinitely loving. Man, on the other hand, falls incredibly short of God's perfection. I myself probably have accrued millions of blemishes on my record, counting both actions and thoughts. Our imperfections create an interesting dilemma in the spiritual realm.

God set up all the laws with perfect justice in mind. So what happens if one of God's children, whom he loves infinitely, violates a law that requires a severe penalty? In order to be loving, God must want to see the person exonerated, but in order to execute justice, he must require the full punishment for the violation. Let's say it is a crime punishable by death. How can God allow the person he loves to keep on living for even a second longer once the person has committed this sin? If perfection is God's standard, we should all be banished from his presence.

This is the dilemma that God has (which he anticipated). He has to enforce his rules to the full extent, but he wants to show his love. So how on earth can he do both at the same time? How can he give everlasting love and capital punishment to the same person?

I remember the scariest day of Jenna's existence—for me. It started out with a regular trip to my in-laws' for some grub. Before the meal began, we were outside playing Frisbee with Jenna, as was typical. On this particular occasion, we noticed the neighbor's pet, a thicker boxer-type dog, loafing around the corner of my in-laws' unfenced yard. She meandered over to Jenna, and the sniffing began; no big deal. Well, it wasn't a big deal until the neighbor's other dog—a larger, more muscular, and very possessive male boxer-type named Henry—noticed what was going on in our yard. In no time, he had slipped his collar and was making a mad dash toward Jenna.

My father-in-law, my wife, and I had been throwing the Frisbee from the back deck, which is where we were standing when we spotted the charging Henry. At that point, I had never seen him before, but I knew this was not going to be good. Henry was crazy and aggressive, and Jenna is a lover, not a fighter. Henry's momentum took him right into fight mode, but Jenna figured out what was going on before he could strike. Both dogs reared up on their hind legs, clawing furiously at each other. They bared their teeth, growling and biting ferociously at each other's faces. All of this happened before we observers could even move.

I've heard it said that you should never get between two fighting dogs, but my concern for Jenna quickly superceded that rule. I didn't know who this enemy dog was or where he had come from, but I was not going to stand for his attacking *my* pup. As fast as we could, all three of us previously frozen spectators jumped onto the scene. By the time we got to the tangling dogs—seconds—my worst fear had already been confirmed. Henry had his strong jaws clamped on poor Jenna's neck. She was trying helplessly to resist.

First I tried to grab a handful of Henry's scruff and pull him off. No luck. Then I tried to clamp my hand around his windpipe, with still no result. By that time, my father-in-law, my wife, the neighbor, and I were all involved in the scrap, trying to pry the dogs apart. I noticed that Jenna started to bleed from her neck, and that was the last straw. I wrapped my arm around Henry's neck and started to choke him out completely. I was concerned that he would turn his head and bite at me, but I had to free Jenna at any cost. Finally, the vicious attacker let go of Jenna, and the neighbor pulled him by his hind legs back to their house.

We quickly attended to Jenna's injuries, which weren't much more than a few small puncture wounds around her neck and ears. She remained good-natured as ever while we fixed her up, oblivious to the seriousness of the encounter. We found out later that Henry had a brain tumor, which may have been responsible for his over aggressiveness. He had to be put to sleep shortly after that episode.

It didn't really matter to me how Jenna got involved in this potentially fatal conflict. I was concerned with only one thing: getting her out. I knew that none of my commands made a difference at that point—they couldn't save her. I knew that a tactical assault on Henry was not going to happen. There was only one thing I could do in this dilemma. I had to put my own skin on the line for her. I had to get personally involved if I wanted to save Jenna from death.

Death hangs over our human heads here on earth. Certainly physical death is frightening, but spiritual death is much more devastating. Physical death in inevitable because our physical organs will eventually fail. But spiritual death is the result of spiritual failure. We talked about human failures—mine specifically—back in the early chapters. The first step in forming a relationship with God is realizing that we have these shortcomings. As we understand more about God and his perfect nature, we realize just how glaring these shortcomings are, especially to the perfect judge. These shortcomings cannot be overlooked by a God with justice in mind. A penalty must be paid. We like to rank our faults—"Oh, that one isn't so bad,"—but every single one of them disqualifies us from perfection. Every one of them forces a wedge between the human and God.

This wedge may not be obvious in the physical world (though it will become so). In the spiritual world, however, this wedge is immovable by man. We remain separated from the loving Father every time we fail to live up to perfection. And there's nothing we can physically do to earn back God's favor. Each and every human is signed up for the penalty for their failures. That penalty, which is required to "re-perfect" the system, is our removal from the system altogether. If God can tolerate only perfection, an imperfect humanity has no hope. Removal by death is the only recourse God has for a fallen man. Death on all levels—physical, emotional, and spiritual—is the sentence for our sins. It must be executed in order for justice to prevail.

The God of the universe—all knowing, all powerful, and all just—saw that humanity's death was inevitable. Like Henry, death was barreling right for us at full speed. So God gave us some commandments, but that didn't seem to help us to evade death. He set up some brilliant battle parameters, but death was still coming strong. The final consequence of our failures was right at the front door, ready to take us down. There was only one thing God could do to stop death from consuming his beloved children. He had to step into the middle of the fight himself. He had to put *his* skin on the line.

So God became a man. I know it sounds weird to hear it like that. God decided that *he* would take the penalty for *our* failures on himself. Humanity had failed, and humanity had to be punished, so God had to become human if he was to take on our death sentence. By the spiritual laws God had put into place, this was the only way to save us. He had to set foot upon earth physically. And no doubt, if you live in America, you've heard of the man that was (and is) God—the one known as Jesus Christ.

I'm saying all of this matter of factly, which is how it is often conveyed by believers. Granted, these are the facts, as spelled out in the manual God has preserved for us, but that doesn't make it any easier to believe. No, it doesn't make sense from a scientific view. Yes, it does require faith. But if we ever hope to get on good terms with God simply because we can philosophize, we are barking up the wrong tree. Humankind's intelligence has taken us to new places, but it has never been powerful enough to defeat death even in the physical realm. Only God can do that. To connect with him will always require an element of faith. To grow in him is to grow this faith.

As I've mentioned before, I like things practical. I like them in black and white. *Faith* continues to be a nebulous term, and in itself it doesn't tell me how I can get closer to God. I can't tell if my faith rating is two out of ten or eight out of ten. Heck, the scale may be out of one hundred; I don't know. Fortunately, God was kind enough to give us a benchmark. He tells us exactly how much we have to believe in order to jump from theorization about him to a relationship with him. He tells us exactly how much faith we need to avoid spiritual death.

The simplest explanation of how we can truly and officially begin a relationship with God is found in Acts 16:31. Paul explains that all we must do is "believe in the Lord Jesus Christ, and you will be saved" (NIV). The benchmark for relationship with God is moving past a general belief in a distant God to a belief in the integrity of his Bible to a belief in Jesus the Savior. We have to believe in Jesus—that the work he did here on earth is sufficient to save us.

So what exactly *did* Jesus do on earth? Well, to start simply, he was born a baby just like the rest of us. His birth through the Virgin Mary is the reason for the Christmas season. Jesus grew into a good man, spreading God's word throughout the region of ancient Israel. He was a revolutionary teacher, though his simplistic teachings often ruffled the feathers of the religious types in authority. Jesus gave evidence of his divinity through the miracles he performed, healing and helping the less fortunate. The Bible spells it out quite clearly in the New Testament. Jesus is the "Son of God," which illustrates his unbreakable connection to God—in nature they are one in the same. Jesus came to earth and showed us the true nature of the God we serve.

But that isn't all Jesus did on earth. Showing up and firing off a few miracles was not sufficient to save mankind from impending spiritual death. To save us, Jesus had to meet a few requirements. He first had to live without any moral or spiritual failure. If Jesus sinned, then he would deserve punishment, just like each one of us does. His death would then be warranted. The Bible tells us that he did not sin, and therefore he was qualified to take the punishment intended for another (Hebrews 4:15). Jesus's perfect life did not go unnoticed by the people. Some figured out that he was God with skin on and rightfully followed him. Others—primarily the self-centered traditionalists—did not like how his teachings chafed them. They eventually decided that he and his teachings would have to be eliminated.

They decided on a bit more than just simple elimination. They wanted total humiliation. They wanted ultimate agony. They wanted the world to see him die. So they called for his crucifixion—the most brutal way for an offender to die in ancient times. Jesus was stripped of his clothes, beaten to a pulp, and then hung on an execution stake—the cross—for the world to see. This innocent, perfect man, the platonic son of God, was killed in a grossly unjust spectacle in front of the entire city of ancient Jerusalem. He stepped into our dogfight and got eaten alive…or so it seemed. But three days later, Jesus offered his followers yet another evidence of his divinity when he defeated death's grip and appeared before them alive. Not a tough accomplishment—if you're God.

I don't make the spiritual laws, so I don't know exactly how it works "scientifically." But I do know that we need to be saved from death, and I know that God wants to save us, and I am willing to accept whatever method he wants to use to do this. The Bible is explicit—*Jesus* is the way. Faith in him is the only hope for me, and you, and a world filled with failure. We can't philosophize or earn our way into salvation; we can only *accept* Jesus's amazing sacrifice. He took our failures upon himself and paid our price for us so that we would not have to experience spiritual death and eternal separation from our loving Father. He proved that he owned death by rising from the grave.

If you need to be assured that you accept God's way to save us—Jesus—then just tell him that. He's always as close as a prayer. There is a salvation prayer included on page 293 of this book, which works just fine if spoken in sincerity. The point is simply that we must let God lay down the rules, especially in the realm of the spiritual. If we want to connect with him, we have to do it on his terms. We can know everything there is to know about God, but unless we insert our faith, we are nothing more than data repositories. God didn't step into the dogfight to gain extra mental megabytes of biblical storage space. He stepped into the dogfight so we could be his friends, his family, and his legacy here on earth.

Knowledge and Enthusiasm

Earlier in this book, I touched on two possible ways a person can react to a relationship with God. This book follows one of the reaction types, which includes a lot of reasoning and an eventual conclusion that Jesus is the God-given answer to life's destructive tendency. My faith grew slowly, but it was reinforced by the truths I understood at each turn. In other words, I did not move much into friendship with God until I fully understood that he was the boss. I did not fully grasp him as my Savior until I understood him to be my loving Father. I continue to build my relationship and my faith block by block, and with each advance my enthusiasm for God grows.

The other reaction type is instant faith and enthusiasm. This method jumps ahead to accepting Jesus as Savior with the child-like faith that is essential to a relationship with God—and that's where the enthusiasm kicks in. Realizing that the God of the universe cares for each of us individually is quite a discovery, especially when a person is feeling lower than dirt. Whereas my path to Jesus was more of a process, the second method is often a dramatic change. This change must then be maintained through a building up of biblical knowledge so the faith-inspired position can be better understood.

The long and short of it is that knowledge alone gets you nothing, and enthusiasm alone gets you nothing. Both play their appropriate roles in the development of faith. If you are enthusiastic about God, great! Learn about him. If you are educated about God, great! Get excited about what he's done for you. The journey toward God always includes faith in Jesus, and it always includes knowledge of the character of God. God wants his people to be well rounded, not lopsided. It is the lopsided believers who can give Christianity a bad name.

The Bible tells us in Romans that "the wages of sin is death, but the gift of God is eternal life through Jesus Christ our Lord" (Romans 6:23, KJV). That pretty much sums it up. We all have both a paycheck and a gift waiting for us at the end of this lifetime. The paycheck—what our pathetic efforts have earned for us—is death. The gift that God wants to give us is life, to an extent that we don't even yet fully understand. All we have to do is accept the gift before we receive the paycheck.

God sees us struggling down here on earth, just like I saw Jenna struggling with Henry. I didn't get involved because of obligation or personal gain. I got involved because I love Jenna as if she were my very own flesh and blood. That is why I put my neck on the line to save her. The Bible tells us that "greater love has no one than this, that one lay down his life for his friends" (John 15:13, NASB). This level of love exceeds friendship and even fatherhood. This is the level of love God has for us. This is why Jesus stepped out of heaven to become our Savior. I can conceptualize God's wisdom, his power, and even his benevolence. But why he has such love for a failing human race is the real mystery to me. Fortunately, I don't have to understand it all. I just have to believe it.

> For God so loved the world, that he gave his only begotten Son, that whosoever believeth in him should not perish, but have everlasting life.
>
> John 3:16 (KJV)

The Tumor

I talked about Jenna and Henry's dogfight in the last chapter and how it scared the daylights out of me. What a sad thing to see my favorite pup in the world threatened by possible death in the jaws of another dog. I was pretty angry with Henry as the situation played out, but afterward, I started to feel sorry for him. Jenna was okay, but Henry was not. Sure, he didn't sustain any injury in the fight, but he had a tumor growing on his brain that likely caused his malevolence. Jenna got away with a few scratches, but Henry's condition was fatal. Neither Jenna nor Henry, however, will ever truly understand this.

Can you imagine trying to explain a brain tumor to a dog? Jenna might be able to understand to some ultra-basic extent an external injury to another dog. She might see blood and try to help lick the wound. But she will never comprehend something working internally—something evil—that is destroying a neighbor dog from the inside out. She may have figured out that Henry in his insanity was trying to kill her, but she will never know the reason behind his attack—the source of the mental imbalance. Jenna can understand the *results* of the tumor, but not the tumor itself.

Humanity has similar limitations in our understanding of death. We can see the results of death, a literal or figurative corpse, but we tend to misinterpret its source. Often we blame God for the existence of death, but it really comes down to choice. We've talked about death being the legitimate penalty for our failures, and that by choosing to accept Jesus, we are choosing life. Not choosing Jesus, on the other hand, results in spiritual death, as well as eventual death on other levels. God cannot be blamed if we decide to choose death, even if it is a choice made in ignorance. This being the case, we often blame God for giving us a choice. Why didn't he set this world up so we *all* get spiritual life?

There would be no point in having options if all the options were the same. When we are presented with two choices, there is always a better choice and a worse choice. The life that each of us has right now is the result of two things: our circumstances and how we choose to react to them. God has control over the circumstances, and we've already talked about his motives. The Bible tells us that he doesn't want anyone to die, but he does want each of us to turn from our wrong ways (2 Peter 3:9). So we know God is moving our circumstances around in a way that will help us to make the right choice. In other words, circumstances are already in the favor of God's children. The only area of question is our reaction to those circumstances. This is where our part—our choice—comes into the picture. If we choose to act in a way that is in line with God's program, we will see new life in our being. If we choose to act in a way that is against God's plan, how can we blame him when we fall?

Get Out of the Way!

My dad used to take our family dog, Molly, with him when he jogged. Molly loved it. The problem was that she didn't understand my dad's goal to run X number of miles that day. Molly couldn't grasp the whole point of the program. Instead, she saw an opportunity to run and play with my dad. In her ignorance, much of the time Molly stopped or slowed right in front of my dad. He was, in turn, forced to slow up or side step her. As a result, his mission of however many miles that particular day was hindered. Molly had no idea she was hurting his goals.

Well, Molly's ignorance didn't last long. My dad decided that he was not going to compromise his running stride no matter what she did. That meant that if she was in the way, she was getting stepped on or kicked. My dad's mission was far more important than Molly's comfort. A few scrapes and bruises later, Molly had learned a valuable lesson and never slowed my dad down again. From that point forward, jogging went much smoother for both of them.

God has a mission here on earth: to build relationships with his children. Oftentimes we don't understand this truth or grasp it fully. But if we start getting in the way of God's mission, there is a great chance we are going to be stepped on. His mission is much more important than our comfort, and, honestly, even our lives. To think any differently is to be prideful.

So we have a choice. We can run alongside God's program, or we can selfishly fight against it. If we choose to fight it—to obstruct God's mission—we can't be surprised if we get stepped on. In fact, we should *expect* to be removed. In the end, everything that stands against God will be crushed. This is why we must choose to stand on the right side in the battle. Bad things happen not because God wants them to happen; they happen because man foolishly stands in God's way. By this stance, mankind often chooses death.

Why Choice?

So why did God place this weighty choice in the hands of mere mortals? Why do we have the choice to run beside him or be squashed? Because of his love. In the last chapter, we talked about God's love and his justice. God's love motivated a plan to save us from a justifiable death. In other words, God's love is superior to his desire for instant justice. In this chapter, God's love and his power face off. Certainly God has the power to control all of my actions if he wanted to. If he would like to make me punch myself in the stomach, there's nothing my petty muscles can do to stop him. Yet instead of controlling me like a robot, he decided to give me a choice. I can choose to enter into a relationship with him, or I can choose not to.

Without choice, there is only automation. I enjoy how my computer or my car or my TV works, but I would be a fool to genuinely *love* them. I would be an even bigger fool to expect them to love me back. It's like the difference between Jenna and one of those toy robo-dogs. The robo-dog will never "love" me any more than the day I pull it out of the package. Jenna, on the other hand, has the capacity to build a relationship with me. The reason we *can* build a relationship is because we both have a choice *not to*. Jenna could refuse me and I could refuse her. But because we *choose* to connect with each other, love can develop.

God had the choice between a people who could walk through the motions forever and a people who could genuinely love him but might screw up too. He had the power to have either, but love motivated him to choose the latter. His love outranks his power in this conflict. And with his choice to give us choice came our options. We get to choose how we react to an often-harsh environment. We get to choose to enter into a relationship with God or not.

Here's a news flash: Historically we've chosen the wrong option. In fact, even from creation, man has set his course toward making poor choices. When God made the universe, it was perfect. God actually *did* set up the planet in a way that everyone could have life and not death. Man, however, chose to mess it all up, as the Bible tells us. God and man had a wonderfully unhindered relationship by design. But then man chose to do the wrong thing. Of course, he didn't realize the implications; he just did what felt right. The death in the world we see today is the result of his and our continued choices to step in the way of God's mission.

Another Invisible Force

Mankind's poor choices are largely responsible for the death we see in the world. But there are other forces at work, as there were even in Adam and Eve's time thousands of years ago. Specifically, there is an evil force—a tumor—that prowls the planet, looking for victims. Adam and Eve were his first, but certainly not his last. This tumor of the spiritual realm was also given a choice long ago whether or not he would maintain a relationship with God, and he chose not to. Now this spiritual cancer tries to slowly destroy mankind by influencing us to make the same wrong choice.

The tumor chose to oppose God, and he is still paying the price. This evil tumor is none other than God's arch-nemesis, the devil himself. Whereas believing in God can give a warm fuzzy, thinking about a purely evil character can have the opposite effect. For this reason many people choose to believe that the devil doesn't exist. But denial is no way to get rid of a tumor, and humanity has all the symptoms. Sometimes the devil's influence on our world seems more apparent than God's.

God didn't give us the desire to kill each other, yet we see wars and murders all around us. God didn't originate the idea of famines and lack, yet we see nations starving to death. God certainly didn't think it would be fun to introduce disease to humanity, yet millions on our planet have fatal diseases. This is not the handiwork of a loving God. This is the deception and destruction of an evil enemy. Many of these tragedies result from man's often-unknowing cooperation with the enemy in opposing God's mission. We've been deceived into choosing to go against God.

How does this deception work? Simply by appearance. When I looked, for example, at the fight between Henry and Jenna, I saw one dog that was a winner and one dog that was a loser. Big, tough, iron-jaw Henry made short work of my poor, wimpy, gentle-natured dog. Jenna left the fight beaten and bloodied and really was only able to survive because of human intervention. If I knew a second go round was inevitable, I would certainly hope for Jenna, but would put my money on Henry. He was the undisputed victor.

But wait a minute. There isn't going to be another bout because Henry is dead. The tumor in his brain was determined to be fatal and he therefore had to be put to sleep. The poor guy is forever in his grave now. Jenna, on the other hand, is alive and well today. She still loves to play fetch and sniff other dogs. She looks to be set up for a long life of love and enjoyment. Jenna will leave a legacy in our household. That dogfight is in her distant past; I doubt she can even remember it.

So maybe Henry didn't win after all; he just *looked* like the winner in the short term. In the long term, his condition consumed him. The tumor might have made him aggressive and fearless, but in the end it brought him down. He isn't the winner at all. Wimpy old Jenna is.

In the world, it looks like the devil is winning sometimes—successfully infecting the human race. But his victory is only in the short term. Choosing the devil's way—the tumor—may give some initial pleasures or benefits, but in the long term, it is sure to fail. Death is the end result. If we are only willing to look at life through our physical eyes, we are very likely to be deceived.

The Bible tells us, "Be careful! Watch out for attacks from the devil, your great enemy. He prowls around like a roaring lion, looking for some victim to devour" (1 Peter 5:8, NLT). And while the devil seeks to consume us, no one is going to knowingly go toe to toe with a lion. We usually have to be lured in, tricked into a trap that we can only see once it is too late. Certainly we can walk around ignorant or unbelieving of the devil's power, but once we are consumed, it is too late to walk in line with God.

Death in an Herb?

One of the enemy's deceptions that infected my life was drugs—specifically marijuana. You see, the first time I inhaled, I didn't fall down dead. In fact, I felt pretty good. At that point, I could take it or leave it, but with the encouragement of that good feeling, I decided to take it…a lot. And slowly the effects became noticeable.

I became lethargic, little by little. I lost motivation. I wasted money. I grew dependent on the feeling the drug provided. I became more connected to alcohol and more willing to try other drugs. My morals sank lower and lower. I eventually went into a depression in which I started to feel like death was approaching. In fact, in my depraved condition, I started to welcome the thought of death. I started to consider assisting death in its process in my life. And it could all be traced back to an "innocent" puff.

Death started to become so painfully real to me—so viable and tangible. I could almost feel the icy breath of death behind me as I pondered suicide. Death was the way I understood this sinister feeling. Death was the label I had given my misery. But in reality, death was only the end result of a depressive tumor infecting the inside of me. Death was all I could understand, but pure evil was the force behind my condition. God's enemy, the devil, was doing all he could to win the battle for my life. He sure wasn't using a cute little pitchfork though.

The devil wants to take me down, just like he wants to take you down. He almost succeeded in my life, and chances are, at some point he's almost succeeded in yours. I needed a way out of my sadness, and I needed it fast. Fortunately, as you have already read, I turned my attention to God, and he slowly helped me out of that particular battle with his nemesis. God showed his saving power by pulling me out of my pit.

The devil is real, and he is scary, but we shouldn't let ourselves get caught up on that. God is bigger and stronger than the devil and any other problems that can come at us. God wants to be our Savior; he wants to save us from the minor stresses of the day, as well as from eternal death. He wants to help us through our anguish. Remember, God not only has the facts, he has the experience. He wants to help us so badly that he stepped onto this planet as a mere mortal and faced the devil's deadly onslaught in the same manner that we have to every day. God has been there, and he has showed us that victory is possible. In the middle of the dogfight, facing certain death, Jesus never lost sight of his mission on earth. And even though it looked like he was defeated—that God had lost—we all know how illogical that is. In the end, God will emerge victorious. In fact, he's already emerging, if we can look beyond the devil's deception. As long as we are running *with* God's program, and not *against* it, we can be assured that salvation is on the way.

Inside the unfathomable mind of God is *all* knowledge, including what it is like to go through human struggles and how to triumph over them. As we grow closer to God, we grow closer to victory over anything the devil can pitch our way. The evil we experience assures us that the devil is alive and working on this planet. The love of God, evident through his salvation power, helps remind us that the devil's time is short. The tumor might look like he's winning, but he's not. This disease is only fatal if we let it be. As long as we cling to God's perfect cure—Jesus—spiritual health is on the way.

> Here on earth you will have many trials and sorrows. But take heart, because I have overcome the world.
>
> —Jesus
>
> John 16:33b (NLT)

Choosing Sacrifice

God is a loving force, drawing us closer to him so the relationship can be born and developed. It is reassuring to think about a loving Father guiding our lives behind the scenes. The concept of God gives us that warm fuzzy for which we often search, which is why churches often stress the blessings and downplay the hardships. But as I have mentioned before, the Christian lifestyle is no walk in the park. Granted, God is the most rewarding pursuit we can undertake, both in theory and in practicality. But walking the way he wants us to walk can be a battle of epic proportions. It might—no, it *will*—take everything we've got to get through it.

Jesus mentions many times in the Bible that there will be intense struggles ahead. Accepting him as Savior doesn't magically change life into a cakewalk. Understanding the existence of the devil helps reveal why the hardships come. Not only is God a mighty force pulling us toward him with his love and saving grace, but there is another strong force that stands in complete opposition to God. That means if God wants you to do one thing, then the devil wants you to do the complete opposite. If God wants you to go to church, then the devil wants you to stay at home. If God wants you to read the Bible, the devil will do all he can to keep you from opening that book. God is at work in your life right now, but so is the tumor.

Before I started to seriously seek after God, I never really looked at things that way. In fact, that way of thinking seemed to be a bit over-spiritual to me. I was well aware of the power of choice; I had fought tooth and nail to obtain this power from my parents. Once I was able to choose my own destiny, I started to see that my choices had a drastic effect on my past, present, and future. Choice was even more powerful than I had initially surmised. At that point, I didn't understand that choice was a gift from God, given with the hope that I would choose him. I saw only the addictive power of choice, and I focused my energy on making choices to maximize fun and minimize responsibility. I made my choices for *me*.

Not surprisingly, *me* did not want to go to church on Sundays. *Me* did not want to read the big, boring Bible—ever. *Me* did not want to pray, unless it somehow served *me*. Instead, *me* preferred to get high and drunk. *Me* preferred to call in sick for work. *Me* chose to sleep all day and party all night. I was so incredibly focused on *my* selfish desires and *my* right to choose that I was oblivious to the influences on those decisions. I only understood *my* part of the equation—my choice. I didn't understand that certain circumstances were quite easily herding me into those wrong choices. A certain force was prodding me along toward intoxication and eventual devastation. This force did not have my best interest at heart, as my depression would soon verify. This force was definitely *not* God.

Every Sunday, I had the choice to go to church or not. Even though I figured God probably wanted me there, I usually used my choosing power to not go to church. Part of me wanted to be a member of a caring congregation, but instead I chose to stay in bed. My tiredness, or hangover, or "busy schedule" outranked the desire to go to church. At the same time, I thought there was some merit to having that small desire to do the right thing. I thought that because I had a conscience, I must have been on God's good list. My power was in my ability to choose, and my ace in the hole was the fact that I had a base understanding of right and wrong.

We've talked about faith and love being dead without action, and we've talked about "working" for God. When right and wrong present themselves, our obligation is not simply to distinguish them. We have to *act* on them—put in some work. But sometimes our course is even harder than token community service. Sometimes choosing to do the right thing for God has great personal cost.

I talked about Jenna's fetch-related injury in an earlier chapter and how much it grieved me to see her hobbling around all mopey. At the same time, happiness sprung up inside me when she decided to get up and wish me goodnight even through her hurt. Jenna provided me with a tangible expression of her love for me that night. And of course I gave her as much extra affection as I could. I knew what she did wasn't easy—heck, it wasn't even expected. I knew her decision to come see me had a price tag of a certain amount of pain. And I knew she decided that seeing me was more valuable than her comfort. Jenna chose to sacrifice her comfort for me, and it meant the world to me.

I could have learned a lot from Jenna if I had her around years earlier when I was going through my drug struggles. On Sunday mornings, I was all comfortable in bed, and getting up was a pain. I knew God wanted to see me at church, but I was not willing to sacrifice my comfort for him—at least not early on. I didn't understand what incredible value even this small-scale sacrifice would mean to him and our strained relationship. I didn't grasp that my relationship with God sometimes depended on my ability to sacrifice my comfort to do what he wanted from me. And I didn't even have a good excuse, like Jenna's injury.

As I continuously avoided going to church and many other constructive activities, a slow realization came over me. I thought that my choice was my power, but I realized that by drinking and drugging, I was slowly giving that power away. The part of me that used to be 50 percent for going to church and 50 percent against was growing lopsided. In fact, my attendance over the previous several years had shown that I had become roughly 95 percent against church, Christmas and Easter being the major exceptions. The decision to go to church—the ability to choose—had become an all-out battle. If God wanted me to be there, why was it *so* hard for me to get there?

Certainly the devil was opposing me, but the bottom line is that I was unwilling to sacrifice for God. My addictions, and really, general society, had taught me to use my power of choice for myself and no one else. I was unwilling to say, "Gosh, this is really tough, and I might be bored out of my gourd for a couple hours, but I'm going to do it anyway." I was watching out for number one, and number one was *not* God in my mind.

In 2 Corinthians 6:17-18, the Bible says, "Therefore, come out from them and separate yourselves from them, says the Lord. Don't touch their filthy things, and I will welcome you. And I will be your Father, and you will be my sons and daughters, says the Lord Almighty" (NLT). I know that I had touched a whole lot of filthy things, and it was time for me to be different from the world around me. It was time to separate, and this separation was going to be painful. But it was also time to be welcomed into the open arms of a loving Father and Savior. Was the road going to be tough—filled with personal sacrifice? Yes. But this is God. The road was going to be awfully rewarding too.

Why Sacrifice?

Why does God want us to sacrifice? Because sacrifice demonstrates love, and it happens to be a language God is quite fluent in. It isn't hard for God to give us a million dollars or heal us from cancer or give us a beautiful sunny day—no skin off his back. When you have infinite resources and knowledge, giving a few away to your children is nothing. But there is a way God limited himself for us. He sent his only begotten son to be a sacrifice for us. This was literally skin off God's back.

Jesus only had one time to experience life as a human. He had one shot to experience all the highs and lows of life as mankind lives. If he wanted to experience something, it had to be during those approximate thirty-three years that he was among us. If he wanted to be a millionaire, it had to be in that lifespan. If he wanted to have a human wife, it had to be in that lifespan. If he wanted to party it up, it had to be in that short earthly appearance.

Jesus decided that he only wanted one thing: what God the Father wanted. Driven by love for the race that was killing him, he did not become a millionaire or a husband or a drunkard. He became our ultimate sacrifice. He laid it all down—his comfort, his human potential, his choice, and even his life—so that we would have a chance to be free. He knew it would hurt excruciatingly, but he got up and hobbled over to that cross just like Jenna hobbled over to my side of the bed. Jesus—God incarnate—sacrificed so that *we* could have the choice that is before us today.

We are bought with a price (1 Corinthians 6:20). It wasn't just a freebee for God. He had to pay dearly. And although salvation is free to us, there is also a cost to following God. Sometimes, to reciprocate our love, we have to step out of our comfort zones and do what he wants us to do. It might be as simple as rolling out of bed on a Sunday morning. But it might be tougher. There is a personal cost to separating ourselves from the filthiness we once embraced. We might have to give up things we like and even love.

Great Personal Cost

I had to make some really tough choices in the wake of my substance dependencies. The first several, which I've already detailed earlier, were the practical steps—forcing myself to go to church or read the Bible or pray. But I also had to separate myself from drugs. I had to separate myself from alcohol. I had to separate myself from sexual temptation. And to do so, I had to separate myself from the friends I loved. I sacrificed my comfort so that I could go to church.

I sacrificed my desire as best I could to overcome my addictions. But I essentially sacrificed some of the best friendships I had known so that I had a shot at growing close to God. I just couldn't hang out with them if my intention was to succeed. And the worst part is that they couldn't understand my choice. To many of them, I remain an irrational weirdo to this day.

"How could you abandon your friends?" you might ask, especially if you knew of the many times they had helped me when I was too drunk or high to help myself. But it isn't them I'm abandoning; I can honestly say that most of them are good people. It is the tumor they carry, however, that forced me to put distance between us. The life I live now, characterized by peace and joy, is not a result of the debilitating lifestyle I used to live. It is a result of choosing a different style. I sacrificed that old life with no guarantees, just a hope in God for a new life. I still love those friends, and I wish they would all eventually choose to follow God like I did, but I am happy that I made the trade.

There are three truths that I would like all of my old friends to ingest—three truths that separate our lifestyles. The first truth is that a relationship with God is available to anyone. God doesn't care who you are; you just have to be willing to sacrifice what he wants you to sacrifice. I used to feel like I was unworthy of him, which is correct. The whole human race is unworthy of him, yet he still has relationships with many of us—those who choose him. It doesn't matter how crusty you feel, God wants to connect with you. Worthiness is not a qualification.

The second truth is that life with God is a thousand times better than life without him. Who wouldn't benefit from having a loving Father who is more powerful, wise, and caring than any earthly relative? I used to think the church life was nothing but boredom, but I can assure you that my life is not boring at all. God designed our ability to have fun, and so he has wholesome ways to satisfy it. Not to mention that every other area in my life is better—finances, friends, job, family relations—you name it. He knows how to give us a permanently abundant life.

The third truth is that we don't have to do it alone. When I looked out of my addiction-created hole, I just didn't think I had what it took to get out. I was right. But when I teamed up with God, I had more than enough strength to get through the struggles. Whatever challenge stands before you might truly be too big for you, but it isn't too big for you and God together.

With or without God, the road of life is going to be tough. There will be struggles and persecutions along any path we choose. But choosing God is the only way to a happy ending. We might have to give up friends, family, stuff, and self in order to advance our spiritual well being. We don't necessarily have to give up everything, but we have to be willing to give up *anything*. God lets us know that in the short term, things will be good if we choose him. In the long term, things will get great. In the eternal term, our happiness will be forever secure. I believe what God says.

> And Jesus replied, "I assure you that everyone who has given up house or brothers or sisters or mother or father or children or property, for my sake and for the Good News, will receive now in return, a hundred times over, houses, brothers, sisters, mothers, children, and property—with persecutions. And in the world to come they will have eternal life."
>
> Mark 10:29-30 (NLT)

God's Un-Understandable Plan

Let me ask you something: Have you ever encountered a claim or statement about God that was difficult to believe, perhaps even in this book? How about some biblical information that you just weren't sure about? I know I have. It starts to make me wonder, why all the mystery? Why doesn't God just dump all the truth I need on me right here and now, so I don't have to wonder? He must have a reason that he doesn't reveal everything right now.

And he does. We always have to remember that God wants a relationship founded on trust, not information. I have tons of information about Michael Jordan, including several basketball cards, but I have no relationship whatsoever with the man. I know *about* him, but I don't really know him—there is no foundation of trust between us. God is looking to build our trust in himself, so instead of giving us a data overload, he gives us *opportunities* to choose to trust him—to have faith. Oftentimes, these opportunities come in the form of challenging statements and claims.

When God gives us what we consider to be "unbelievable" information, it isn't so he can stump or confuse us; it is so he can increase our trust in him. It isn't easy to believe in an invisible God, and he knows that. The Bible tells us that we should be walking by faith, not by sight, but most of us do the opposite (2 Corinthians 5:7). We only believe what we can see, and as a result, we don't wholeheartedly believe God at his word. The conclusion is a stunted relationship, if any, and an unfulfilled life. What we see is exactly what we get.

Jenna's typical day is loaded with things she cannot understand. Recently we took her to the vet to get her teeth cleaned; obviously she doesn't grasp the purpose of that. My wife and I were under the impression that such a cleaning would help in her continuing battle with dog breath, but we were sadly disappointed. The only noticeable difference when she got home was a weird-looking shaved spot on her front leg.

I have a pretty hard time sitting still at the dentist, but Jenna has this problem to the hundredth degree. She can't sit still for five seconds, especially with the dental equipment of an unfamiliar doctor in her mouth. Jenna's reaction to a probing stranger is to wriggle her way out of the situation. The poor veterinarian has no choice but to give her a sedative to knock her out for pretty much any medical process. To administer this sedative and other medication, on this particular trip the vet shaved a strip around Jenna's leg and put in an IV. When Jenna returned home from the ordeal, she had standard stinky breath and a bald spot that made her paw look like a plucked chicken wing.

This bald spot got our attention, but it got hers even more. She would not stop licking it, and it started to get raw. So Danielle and I, her unofficial medics, got an old sock and slid it on her leg. We taped it around the top so she couldn't get it off or lick the bald spot any more. Jenna's reaction to her loving parents was in stark contrast to her reaction at the vet's. She just sat there patiently as we performed the procedure that she didn't comprehend. In fact, having that sock on obviously annoyed her, yet she still tolerated the intrusion.

I love Jenna's reaction to the helping hands of Mommy and Daddy. When we put the sock on, to her it was "just another medical procedure." When she cut her foot the other day, and I had to hold her paw and clean it up, it was "just another medical procedure." She wagged her tail through most of it. When Danielle wipes Jenna's dirty paws with the towel, Jenna sees it as "just another medical procedure." Jenna sits patiently and endures nearly every time as we tinker with her injuries or stains.

Jenna might not trust the vet, but she trusts me and my wife unfailingly. Jenna knows we are there to help her, and so she is willing to accept our help. She takes it like a champ every time we have to bandage her or clean her up. She knows we are there to heal her, so she has accepted every one of our "medical procedures" as a worthy interruption to her day.

Honestly, we like to take advantage of Jenna's trusting mentality sometimes. When we dressed her up as a shepherd for last year's Christmas card, Jenna thought it was just another medical procedure. When we rolled her up in a blanket, just for fun, she saw it as just another medical procedure. When we shaved a mohawk into her fur, she thought it was just another medical procedure. Granted, she is always handsomely rewarded with treats after our fun. Part of the reason she is rewarded is her trusting attitude toward her parents. She knows we are her source for good health. She knows we would never do anything to harm her.

We've talked about society's tumor—God's enemy—in the last several chapters. This tumor has done serious damage to society as a whole and to you and me individually. Jesus, however, is the cure for this tumor. But being cured of a disease doesn't necessarily mean that we don't have to go through some rehabilitation. Though our distant future is secured through Jesus's sacrifice (if we accept him), the here-and-now can still require some seriously intrusive medical procedures. Obviously, since none of us is perfect, all of us have improvements to make.

God wants to administer these corrective procedures to us. He wants to see us healed and living to the fullest for our time here on earth. His intentions are not in question, logically speaking. Practically, however, when we do not fully know God or trust him, we tend to do some squirming, like Jenna at the vet. We try to wriggle free from God when there is some pain or discomfort. We only accept the medications *we* approve. By struggling against God, we only make our wholeness that much more difficult to obtain.

Faith is a medicine that God knows will help to develop our lives. Faith is what brought us to God in the first place, and it is what brings us *closer* to God each day. Faith helps us look past what we can see with our eyes to what we know is true about God. We need to walk through life with this faith in God. If we know that God is a good Father and a willing Savior, we should be able to sit still as he administers his beneficial "medical procedures" to us. We should submissively accept whatever he does, as uncomfortable as it may be. He *does* have the power to knock us out if we won't allow him to work. Worse yet, if we are continually resistant, he has the power to stop the medication altogether.

Faith, as valuable as it may be, is not always comfortable to the human mind. As I've mentioned over and over, I am a practical type of guy. That means that what I can touch, taste, and see often ranks a lot higher than my best thoughts or beliefs. It is uncomfortable for me to believe that when I go through struggles, God is still in charge. When I'm caught up in a moment, it is hard to comprehend that God is behind the scenes, working on my behalf.

Faith is what God uses to rehabilitate us from the effects of the devil in our lives. He gives us truths from the Bible, and then he tests how long we will believe those truths. When our faith is weak, we turn away from the Bible at the first place it departs from our "logical" programming. As our faith grows, we become more comfortable with the departures from the visible world. We walk longer and longer, stronger and stronger, as we continue in the truths of the

Bible. When we understand who God is and the relationship we have with him, we can weather tougher and tougher storms. We can sit there patiently as he "intrusively" operates on our lives.

Many of the truths about God continue to challenge our logic, but it is meant to be that way. God wants our relationship with him to be as healthy as it possibly can be, and it is a continual process. I understand and believe a lot more about God today than when I began my pursuit of him. The only way I can continue to grow is to admit that I don't have as much faith today as I want to have tomorrow. There are things I have heard about God or read about God that I may not yet fully believe, but I sure want to. Our relationship with God is not about stubbornly refusing to ever change our beliefs. Our relationship is about continually growing our belief system to match who God shows himself to be. If you believe God is a boss but not a friend, and you keep up your pursuit of him, you will come to know the truth. He wants you to. Seek and you will find (Matthew 7:8).

Trust the Weirdo?

The Bible gives us some prime examples of trusting in God despite appearance. Second Kings chapter five tells about a man named Naaman who was a highly honored army captain. Naaman had a lot going for him; the only problem was that he also had a debilitating disease called leprosy. In Bible times, there was no cure for his condition, so he eventually went to a prophet named Elisha to see if God could heal him. Naaman thought the prophet would wave his hand and say a prayer, and that would be that. He envisioned exactly how God was going to work in the situation. But God had different plans. Elisha had a simple solution for Naaman; he told him to go dip in the Jordan River seven times. Naaman was indignant. He was a man of honor; how could he go wash in such a pathetic little river when there were many other mighty rivers nearby? And seven times, no less. Naaman turned to angrily head home.

Naaman's servant made a comment that stopped his master in his tracks. The servant said, "Sir, if the prophet had told you to do some great thing, wouldn't you have done it? So you should certainly obey him when he says simply to go and wash and be cured." Naaman was willing to do whatever it took to be healed, as long as it fell within *his* parameters. The servant pointed out that Naaman's parameters needed to be expanded to include a "medical procedure" that seemed entirely foolish to the faithless man. Naaman heeded the advice and headed to the insignificant Jordan River to dip seven times. When he came up that seventh time, he was healed of his disease.

It comes down to trust. If I know a doctor who is an eccentric weirdo but has a 100 percent success rate in a condition I had, I am going to look right past the weirdness. I am going to do whatever he tells me to in the medical realm so that I can be healed. I might not understand it all, but I am going to sit there patiently as the medication is administered. I'm going to have faith in his expertise. It's either that or be sick my whole life. I'll choose faith over sickness anytime.

God has both the wisdom and the means to keep us physically, mentally, and spiritually fit. We need to trust in his techniques, no matter how awkward or uncomfortable they are to us. It is true that my wife and I sometimes "take advantage" of Jenna's trusting nature by putting her in a silly costume or giving her a funny haircut. The cost for her is the momentary discomfort, but the payoff is our joy—we have gotten so many laughs out of our relationship with Jenna. If it costs me a little of my comfort to put a smile on God's face, I am all for it. When God smiles, I know good things are coming my way, just like the treats that Jenna gets for her willing participation in our fun. My temporary feelings are a small price to pay for building a relationship with my heavenly Father.

Immortalized

At my desk at work, I have a picture of Jenna wearing an old shirt and tie that we dressed her up in. She has a silly grin on her face—just a dopey look of contentment. I smile every time I look at that picture and think about all the fun we have with her. Even at work she brightens my day because I have immortalized her in that photo. When Jenna is long gone, her silly smile will live on. I will forever enjoy my relationship with Jenna—the trust she has had in me—thanks to my digital camera.

God wants to do more than just smile today—he wants to remember us for a long time. His scale, as you remember, is very long term. Eternal, in fact. And God wants to take the memory of us into eternity with him; he wants to remember us forever. Actually, he wants to do one better. He wants to take *us*, the very essence of who we are, with him into eternity. He wants the relationship with him to last forever, beyond what this frail human body can survive. And the beauty of it is that he has the technology to accomplish this amazing feat.

So how does God do this? No human knows exactly—if we did, we'd probably somehow exploit it. All we can know in *this* life is what we need to do to transition into the *next* life, beginning with Jesus. The Bible tells us that no eye has seen, no ear has heard, and no mind has imagined what God has prepared for those who love him (1 Corinthians 2:9, NLT). That means God has something spectacular planned for his children over the rainbow, so to speak. Even the classic verse, John 3:16, speaks of eternal life. Building a relationship with God begins in this lifetime, but it is not something you do for *only* this lifetime—it is something you can do forever. The only problem is that we don't have forever to *decide*.

Choice is a powerful thing. We have the power to choose God, or not choose God, and our lives will invariably reflect this decision. But there comes a time when we automatically forfeit the ability to decide if we will follow God. That time is death—an inevitable conclusion to life in a corrupted world. Once our lives are over, *God* gets to do the choosing. He chooses whether or not he would like to preserve our relationship forever—whether or not he wants our figurative photos on his desk. He will make this decision based on our relationship with him during this lifetime. Did we accept his cure, Jesus, and the sometimes-intrusive treatment that followed? Or are we simply a product of our feelings and earthly corruption? God is building a heavenly utopia for his children, so he cannot allow those that pooh pooh his plan for salvation and holy living. Otherwise, his utopia would be no different from earth.

Why do I Squirm?

I often have to ask myself, do I really trust God? Do I believe that he wants to give me unimaginably good things? Do I believe he's working to improve me as a person right now? Do I believe that his medicine can help to rehabilitate me from this world's hurtful effects? Do I believe he wants to have an eternal relationship with me? If so, why am I still squirming? If God wants some apparent tragedy to mar my life, why do I get all concerned? I need to just continue to trust him, like my good friend Jenna does me.

The Bible says that hope that is seen is not hope at all (Romans 8:24). You don't have to hope or believe if you have everything spelled out for you. And this is exactly why it isn't. God wants us to build our relationship with him using faith. He has our eternal well-being in mind and can see things from a perspective we can't even dream of. If we can't believe him, then we need to take heavy doses of the practical steps described earlier in this book—church, Bible, and prayer. The more we work at the relationship, the more God will honor our efforts. The more we will see who he really is; our Great Physician.

> It was there at Marah that the Lord laid before them the following conditions to test their faithfulness to him: "If

you will listen carefully to the voice of the Lord your God and do what is right in his sight, obeying his commands and laws, then I will not make you suffer the diseases I sent on the Egyptians; for I am the Lord who heals you."

Exodus 15:25b-26 (NLT)

Anger and Anguish

It makes sense that a perfect, Godly utopia cannot contain murderers, child molesters, thieves, or other unreformed social deviants. In other words, not everyone is going to see the unimaginably wonderful plans God has for their lives and eternities. Some people will choose to live a faithless life, and those without faith cannot build a relationship with God. Those without faith cannot even please God (Hebrews 11:6). And as I've mentioned before, God draws the lines. Once you get to those pearly gates, God decides if you are qualified to enter.

So what if you aren't qualified? What if you have refused or neglected God's explicit cure for the corruption of this world? Well, if God is gathering the things he loves for his heavenly utopia, that means the things he dislikes must be placed elsewhere. We see both good and bad things in the world today, but God is eventually going to take out the trash. Yes, it sounds harsh because there are unfortunately unknowing people included in that trash. But for the sake of his children, God is willing to remove all those things that do not please him. This underscores the importance of working hard *to* please him.

If God can be pleased, this means he can also be displeased. If he can be happy with us, he can also be mad at us. In fact, we've all failed, as we've discussed, so at one time he was unhappy with each and every one of us. If not for his patience, we would have been cast from his presence forever on account of our failure. Fortunately he has offered an alternative to this separation—Jesus. He also has a plan for our continual improvement.

Our relationship with God improves when we behave in a way that pleases him. When we make an effort to draw closer to him, he grows closer to us (James 4:8). But the opposite is true when we do things that displease him. Our relationship is hurt, and he then distances himself from us. A pattern of this behavior causes a separation that becomes eternal if we do not change our ways.

I remember the most hurtful thing Jenna ever did to me and our relationship. Danielle was out of town on an overnight trip, so it was just me and Jenna. Of course, I played with my pup a bunch and tired her out for the night. After a fairly normal evening routine, we both went to bed, me in my normal spot on the bed and Jenna on her comforter on the floor.

In the morning, I woke up before Jenna did. Apparently, she was still tired from playing the night before. As I was walking to the bathroom, I reached down and patted her on the butt and told her, "Good girl," like I normally do. She gave me sort of a bizarre, squinty-eyed look from her prone position. Then, without any real warning, she lunged right at my face, mouth open. Shocked, I jumped back, and her jaws snapped shut not far from my nose. She continued to lie on her comforter, eyeing me up with that strange, remorseless look in her eyes.

At first, I didn't know how to react, but I quickly decided on a course. I first said, "No!" many times over—the standard way of expressing my displeasure. I smacked her several times on her butt, but I did not approach her head because I wasn't sure if she was truly trying to bite me. I ordered her up, which she reluctantly obeyed. With aggressive verbal orders and open displays of anger, I coerced her into another room and shut the door behind her—solitary confinement. I didn't know what had prompted her sudden hostility toward me. I contemplated the direction her decision would take us. I wondered if I was going to have to get rid of the dog I loved.

It turns out that Jenna's main weakness, the area she gets most possessive, is whatever item she has dubbed "her bed." I kind of had a clue from earlier episodes, though this offense took the cake as far as outright revolt. After I cooled off, I let her out of her "cell" and she was just as tail-waggedy and happy as normal—pretty much oblivious to the fact that she had deeply hurt me with her rebellion. Our everyday life slowly returned to the same as before, but Jenna was banned from the bedroom indefinitely.

I have told many people this story, and most of them ask a simple question: "Why did you let her get away with that?" Dogs don't seem to understand much more than brute force, so I am asked why I didn't attack back and let her know who was boss. The answer is simple: because I thought she might bite me. The reason for this answer, however, is not the obvious. I was not *afraid* of Jenna; I've seen her fight, and I know who would win this 105-pound dog vs. 180-pound human clash of the titans. I was more afraid of what *I* would do to Jenna if she seriously attacked me.

If Jenna had somehow decided that she was going to all out attack me, I might not have been left with a choice. I would obviously have had to stop her, and if she became persistent enough, I would have had to use whatever level of force necessary, including lethal force. Now please don't get me wrong; I am not some sort of sadistic deviant. I certainly do not want to hurt or kill the dog I love so much. I am just saying if only one of us is coming out of the ring alive, it's going to be me. I would give Jenna every opportunity to surrender, but if she did not, her fate would be her own.

This is exactly why I kept my distance from Jenna when she tried to bite my face off. I did not want to get into a literal fight with her, and I never do, because I know the end result would not be in her favor. I ordered her away from that bad situation and into solitude so she could re-evaluate her position, and hopefully come out submissive. While this level of analysis may be above her head, my plan still ended up working. We did not have to go toe to toe, and she quickly decided that a happy Daddy is a lot better than a furious one.

God does not want to fight against us because he knows that he will not lose. He knows that if we provoke him enough to take a stand, then we are the ones that will come out of the fight as a smoldering pile of rubble. He knows that if we oppose him for all seventy-or-so of our years on this planet, we're signing our own death warrant. Yet some of us—in fact, all of us, at some point or another—have decided to fight against him. So what is his reaction?

He does exactly what I did with Jenna; he withdraws himself so he won't have to fight. He keeps his distance so he does not have to engage in what will turn out to be a lethal battle…for us. He lets us have our little tantrums and rebellions with the hope that we will reconsider our foolish stance. God knows we are silly humans, prone to flaring outbursts and regrettable snap judgments. He cares about us, so he gives us opportunity after opportunity to get this relationship thing right. But he cannot wait forever. He will not let an aggressive adversary perpetuate ungodliness, especially if it is affecting other people who have chosen to be God's children. Eventually, justice must be executed upon the troublemakers.

On the day that Jenna looked right at me and decided to try to bite me, she took one step down the wrong path. If she decided to stay on this path, there would be only one thing I could do: end this relationship permanently. I absolutely do not ever want to do that, but I am only part of the relational equation. She has her choice, oblivious as she may be, whether or not she wants to be a part of the happiest place she knows—our household. It is a choice that is made every morning when she wakes up and looks at me, a person who has already given her so much. Because I love her, my patience is strong for her, but it is not infinite.

Why is my patience not infinite? Because *she* is not infinite. She only has ten to fifteen years on this earth before she will be gone forever. I wish she could live right alongside me for my entire life, but it just isn't possible in her aging dog body. So Jenna only has those ten to fifteen years to decide if she is going to build a relationship with me or not. If she begins down the path of provoking and fighting me, I might start to get the feeling that she does not want to build a relationship with me. When I become certain of this fact—when she convinces me with her continuous actions that she will never heed my mastership or friendship—then it becomes time for me to stop wasting my time on her. The logical thing to do in this case would be to send her far away from me.

God wants us to be with him for eternity, but because we are not physically infinite either, a decision has to be made during this lifetime. When they die, God's children are going to have it real good. We've already discussed the unimaginable beauty of heaven, not to mention the earthly blessings, for those who pursue God wholeheartedly. But there is another place that people can go when they die. Much like the devil, this place is an unpleasant topic that is often avoided.

The Bible tells us that at the end of time, God is going to separate the "sheep," which are his people, from the "goats," which are those who are not his people (Matthew 25:31-46). Right now, it may be hard to tell who is whom, but it makes sense that God will sort all that out. There are no half-sheep-half-goats in this analogy; people are either one or the other. God is going to make the line obvious, and it might not fall exactly where we think. There will be good people, by human standards, who are not *God's* people. They may have done good deeds, but they might have gone the opposite direction with their hearts or relationship with God. They opposed the scientifically unsatisfactory intangible known as faith. They fought against God, inadvertently as it may have been. And so their choices have caused God to send them away. The final verse of the sheep and goats passage says, referring to those who are not God's people: "And these shall go away into everlasting punishment: but the righteous into eternal life" (v. 46, KJV).

The place we don't want to talk about is this place of eternal punishment—hell. The Bible tells us how horrible it is, but it really doesn't have to for us to understand. God is taking everything good with him into heaven (and its annexes). That means everything bad is going to be in another place. So even if a person "just misses the cut" to get into heaven, that person is going to be put in a place with all the mass murderers, pedophiles, devil worshipers, and other malefactors. Not only that, but all pain, disease, depression, hatred, and every other physical, emotional, and spiritual affliction will be in this place—far from the children of God. I really don't want to talk about this place, but even more than that, I don't want to end up there.

How does this place tie in to a loving God? It is the end result of continuously provoking him. God wants us to listen to him, but he won't force us. If he did, we would no longer have a choice, and love only exists when chosen. How on earth can we blame God for our fate if our only interaction with him is constantly trying to bite his face off? It is inevitable that God's wrath will eventually come thundering down on those who will not be saved. This is the only way justice can be served when dealing with an eternally unrepentant person. It is sad but true.

But there is still time. We can stop our warring with God and avoid the wrath that comes upon those who reject him. God didn't set this planet up so that only the perfect would have a relationship with him. Jesus didn't come to earth to call the righteous people but instead the sinners to repentance (Matthew 9:13). He came to seek and save those that were lost (Luke 19:10). Romans 5:8 says that "God demonstrates his own love toward us, in that while we were yet sinners, Christ died for us" (NASB). That means enemies of God, those currently fighting against him, are perfectly eligible to receive and understand the love of God.

The lines are drawn; God has drawn them. In one hundred fifty years, you and I, the guy next door, the girl at the gas station, and everyone else living on this planet right now will have made their final decision about God. We will all fall on one side of the line or the other. In one hundred fifty years, everyone living today will be in the early years of a very long eternity. I'd say that today is a good time to start preparing for that—at very least, a little. I know I don't want to spend eternity apart from God and all that is good. Even if we are skeptical about heaven, we should know that we don't want to be in hell. God wants us to realize that he loves us, but sometimes our realization of him can start with a healthy fear.

When I wake up in the morning a little grumpy, I'd better think twice about lashing out at the one who decides where I will go. In fact, I'd better be pretty serious about figuring out what he wants me to do *now*. It can be very challenging to live the way God wants us to, but consider the alternative: fighting against God. I don't want to be on God's bad side now, but even more than that, I don't want to be on his bad side *forever*.

> The fear of the Lord is the beginning of wisdom: A good understanding have all they that do his commandments.
>
> Psalm 111:10 (KJV)

> "Yet you have not listened to Me," declares the Lord, "in order that you might provoke Me to anger with the work of your hands to your own harm."
>
> Jeremiah 25:7 (NASB)

Part 7:

God and the Human Spirit: Eternal Laws and Purpose

God the Spirit

As the pursuit of God progresses, we can see just how relationship oriented he is. Often our first impression of God is as a lofty ruler, which is certainly accurate. But he wants to be closer than that. As we keep digging, we begin to see that he is a true friend, accessible to the human race. Yet he wants to be closer than that. Further exploration reveals God's roles as Father and Savior. As we build our relationship with him, we see him getting closer and closer. We understand that he is not only high above, but he is right here beside. It's almost like he gently shrinks down to our level so that we can get a handle on him. Our relationship grows, but one thing stays the same: He *still* wants to get closer.

A couple days after Danielle and I got married, we headed off on the customary honeymoon vacation. Our first stop was Florida for a week and then another week aboard a cruise ship. It was a blast—great weather, non-stop activities, no stresses or worries. There was only one minor problem with the trip: no doggies allowed.

We left Jenna at my in-laws' for the trip, where we knew she would be safe and comfortable, and we really didn't give it much thought. In Florida and on the cruise, Jenna was not forgotten, but she was far from the focus. But back in Michigan, it was a different story. Two weeks was the longest Jenna had ever been without

Mommy or Daddy, and it started to show. While we were gone, she didn't eat as much or as regularly. She didn't sleep as well. She even got just a tad mopey. Often she would stare out the window, hoping that Mommy's red Cutlass Supreme would be the next car to appear on the horizon. After two weeks of hoping, Jenna's ship finally came in.

When we pulled into the driveway after our honeymoon, Jenna could not believe her eyes. She would get pretty amped up when I returned from a two-minute walk to the mailbox, so two weeks must have seemed like a doggy eternity to her. She was beside herself with excitement when we returned. She was also beside *us* for the remainder of the evening, making sure that if that red car left, she was in it. She was resolved to do all she could to make sure she never got separated from us again.

Once we got Jenna back to our apartment, we noticed that she looked a bit skinnier, probably from her no-Mommy-and-Daddy eating disorder. But we also noticed that there was something weird going on with her tail. Normally her tail sticks straight out from her butt and dances around like a flag as she happily prances around. But after our two-week vacation, Jenna's tail had sort of a downward curve, and it wasn't nearly as mobile. It looked like a banana hanging off her butt. At first we laughed at the droopy appendage, but as time went on we started wondering if she had somehow hurt herself bounding around at my in-laws.

Well, apparently our concerns were unwarranted, because in only a few days her wagger was right back to normal whipping status. Soon it was knocking things off shelves and end tables just like it had before. We still don't know exactly what her bizarre "rigor mortis of the tail" was, but we do have a pretty good idea of what caused it. The key exasperator had to be separation from her two best buds in the whole world.

You see, Jenna's life is hopelessly entwined with Mommy and Daddy. To her, life without us is the dumps. Life *with* us cannot be beat. She may forget this from time to time, but deep down, Jenna knows that we are the source of all the good things she has. Maybe it took a few days into our trip for her to realize this. Maybe it only took a few minutes. But after two weeks of painful anxiety and soul searching, Jenna concluded that living life without us would be miserable. Fortunately for her, she doesn't have to worry about that.

The Human Spirit

The Bible tells us in Proverbs that "the spirit of a man will sustain his infirmity; but a wounded spirit who can bear?" (18:14, KJV). Certainly we live in these physical bodies, but there is a lot more to a human being than just flesh and blood. Each one of us also has a mind, which is the center of our thoughts and emotions. But even deeper than that, at our very core, we have something of greater value than our physical or mental capabilities. We each have a spirit. Your spirit is the very essence of who you are.

What this Proverb is telling us, then, is that when we are physically sick—with infirmity—we can cope as long as we retain wellness in our spirit. But if we are defeated deep down, if we have a wounded spirit, it doesn't matter if we are sick or not. We just won't be able to sustain ourselves for very long. If our spirit is in poor condition, the mind and body are sure to follow.

Jenna's tail malfunction is a good example. I'm not going to argue whether or not dogs have spirits, but suffice it to say that Jenna was feeling some deep-down hurt when Mommy and Daddy left her behind. Jenna was in perfect health mentally and physically when we left for the trip. Soon after our departure, some mental symptoms started to kick in with her sporadic eating and sleeping patterns. When Mommy and Daddy didn't show up for an extended period (from her perspective), even her body started to react to the deep internal pain. The end result was the weird saggy, stiff tail Jenna had when we finally returned. Because her "spirit" was crushed, her mind and body started to degenerate.

Spirit Connections

Humankind is used to a variety of relational connections that match our differing depths. At the surface level there are physical connections, typically known for their short duration. Next there are mental and emotional connections between humans, which generally seem to have greater longevity and easily trump any sort of physical bond. Yet mental and emotional connections still have limits in that they are sometimes based on human logic or feeling, both of which can lead us astray. We see physical and mental bonds severed frequently in our disloyal and divorce-ridden society.

But there are deeper connections than those of the body or mind—a type of connection that can sustain even when the other connectors weaken. This is where the human spirit comes into play. A spirit bond cannot be broken simply by physical discomfort or mental anguish. A spirit bond outlasts the other types of connections. A spirit bond is very special, to be sought after and maintained wholeheartedly. A spirit bond is deep—a connection between the essence of one and the essence of another. Not surprisingly, a spirit bond is what God ultimately wants to establish with you and me.

Certainly God appreciates bonds of all varieties; he had a hand in designing each type. God enjoys physical interaction with mankind, which is part of the reason Jesus came to earth. God enjoys mental interaction with humanity, which is in large part what this book is meant to provoke. God is a thinker and a designer, so he enjoys the creativity and ingenuity that he sees in humankind. He even likes to see our emotions, encouraging us to love or persevere. But there is more that he is looking for. He is deeper than the physical and mental, and so are we. He wants to connect to us Spirit to spirit. He knows that our spirits are what carry us through the tough physical, mental, and emotional times. Armed with this knowledge, God wants to work with us extensively at the spirit level.

The majority of churches I've attended have used the phrase "the Father, Son, and Holy Spirit" regularly throughout the service. This concept of God, which is entirely biblical, is known as *the Trinity*. While some of the doctrine behind it can get pretty complex, the gist is that God has three equal "persons" who make up who he is. The Father is the thinker and planner aspect of God, much like the mind is the thinker of man. God the Father is best understood as having the presidential, boss-like, and even fatherly traits discussed in this book. God the Son is Jesus, the physical manifestation of God. He would be best seen as a loving friend and Savior. But deeper yet (not better, just deeper) is the Holy Spirit, who is more of "the essence" of who God is. It is the Holy Spirit aspect of God that forms the deep spiritual connection we need to fully link up with him. The Holy Spirit helps us to develop our connection with God at the deepest level.

Developing a Spirit Connection: Steps One and Two

There is a three-step process to establish and develop a Spirit-to-spirit connection with God. The first step is to be born. I'm pretty sure most readers out there already have this step out of the way. God is our Creator, and that means he has designed us just how he wants us. When we were born, he put within us a natural inclination toward relationships, and specifically, to a relationship with him. In other words, we all have this prerequisite for a spirit bond with God. Referencing unbelievers, the Apostle Paul says in Romans, "They demonstrate that God's law is written within them, for their own consciences either accuse them or tell them they are doing what is right" (2:15, NLT). We all have a moral compass bestowed at birth, which is essentially an internal connection to the things of God. Though circumstances can manipulate and damage our consciences, we all still have natural parameters in which we live.

The second step in establishing and developing a Spirit-to-spirit bond with God is to *be born again*. That's the churchy way of saying we accept the gift of grace through Jesus Christ. As we discussed earlier, the Bible lays it out pretty plainly that Jesus is the way to God. Being born again is a rebirth in our spirit—a time when we recognize that we need a Savior and accept Jesus as just that. There is no other way to entirely fulfill the inclinations we are humanly born with. There is no other cure for a wounded spirit—just temporary treatments. God wants to "shrink down" for us so that we can get a grasp, but he wants to go farther. He wants to work on the *inside* of us, which means we have to let him in. Accepting Jesus gives God the okay to work inside of us. It gives him access to our hearts and consciences.

The conscience is something that can be altered. Though it generally starts out relatively pure when we are children, life can jerk it around pretty good. Soon there is no longer black and white, but lots and lots of gray area. Take, for example, the hot-button issue of abortion. If you explain abortion to a child—without biasing the explanation—I believe the natural reaction would be opposition. In fact, the natural reaction of the United States of America one hundred years ago would have been against. Abortion used to be wrong, no questions asked. But wait; let's throw in some circumstances. What if a mother is lazy and just doesn't want another kid? Abortion doesn't seem right for that situation. What if a mother is concerned that she doesn't have the resources to give a child a decent life? Abortion still seems wrong there, but perhaps less so. What if a woman is raped, and pregnancy is the result? "Well, maybe there should be exceptions, but just for really tough circumstances like that," we as a society start to think. And a social conscience that years ago would have entirely rejected abortion starts to slowly allow a few under extenuating circumstances. Then we start to allow a few more, perhaps for the "caring-but-low-resource mother." The next thing we know, we wake up one morning and abortion is an optional medical procedure, available to anyone. Our social conscience has been altered.

At a personal level, we have all made compromises in our consciences based on circumstance. We have all done things that we knew were wrong deep down, but we somehow justified in our minds. The problem is not necessarily with the one-time mistakes for which we ask and receive forgiveness. The problem is when a mistake develops into a pattern of moral compromise. Generally, nobody seems to care if you take a paperclip from work, probably not even your employer. But if you start with a paperclip, then snag a pen, then a notepad, then a ream of paper, then a computer, you are treading on dangerous ground. Your conscience, which may have stopped you from stealing a computer on day one, has suddenly been convinced that swiping a computer is no big deal. Only bad things will happen if the stealing becomes habitual.

But you see, this is why we need to connect with God at the deepest level. My human conscience has been ravaged by circumstance since childhood, so I need to base my decisions on something a bit more stable. I can't trust politicians or society or friends or even my feelings to tell me what is right and wrong—all of them are too circumstantial. I need to know what God thinks about things, not only because he is the most stable thing going for humanity, but also because when it comes down to the final decision about my life and eternity, his is the only opinion that matters. The bottom line is that individually and socially, we need to get back to what the thoughts of God are in *every* matter. And God doesn't feel any differently about stealing or abortion than he did on the first day of planet earth's existence.

Developing a Spirit Connection: Step Three

Finding out what God thinks leads us into step number three of developing a Spirit-to-spirit link with God. The first step is to be born, and the second step is to be born again. The third step is simply to obey. This step begins with some of the basic tools we've already talked about—the Bible, church, prayer, and good deeds. As we read and understand the Bible, we get a better feel for who God is and what he wants from us. We learn (or affirm) that we aren't supposed to murder or steal or hate. We learn that we are supposed to help and love and give. As we use the tools, putting action to our faith, we grow our connection with God. His morals become stronger on our inside, and we develop the ability to see, at least generally, what God says about many of those gray-area items in our consciences. Circumstances may still affect us, but not as much the more rooted we are in God's morals.

If we let God be the director of our individual spirits, he can show us how to *handle* circumstances. He can show us how to obey in every situation. When we accept the Spirit-to-spirit link afforded by Jesus, we are left with a momentous question: where do I go from here? The answer, which is "closer to God," may not sound very practical at all. Some of the religious staples I can understand—the Bible, the church, prayer—but there are also serious unknowns. *How much* should I read the Bible? *Which church* should I attend? What is an *acceptable* amount of prayer? As a matter of fact, how am I going to pay the bills? What job or promotion should I apply for? What city should I live in? Who should I marry? How does all this Christianity apply to real life? Though the Christian faith offers guidelines and advice in each of these areas, there is no passage of scripture that will specifically tell you, "Thou shalt read four chapters of your Bible per day," or, "Thou shalt go to Mount Hope Church," or, "Thou shalt work as a truck driver." So how on earth can we know what God wants us to do in these every-day situations?

The answer is found in relationship, not religious custom. First Corinthians 2:11 says, "For who among men knows the thoughts of a man except the spirit of the man which is in him? Even so the thoughts of God no one knows except the Spirit of God" (NASB). God has a specific plan for you—a specific church, occupation, companionship, and so much more—that will yield the best possible outcome for your life. Only God has the complete version of this information, and he keeps it exactly where you would expect a loving Father to have his child's best interest: in his thoughts. Granted, we know mentally that God doesn't want us to be thieves or murderers, but to get down to the details of our particular missions in life, we have to link up with his Spirit. We have to have the essence of God imprinted on the inside of us.

The only way to fully maintain wholeness in spirit is to be in relationship with God. That way, when circumstances shake our world, we don't have to go on a religious pilgrimage to try to gain some semblance of peace. If we are in relationship with God, the answers to our struggles abide on the inside of us. *Specific* answers. These answers will be in harmony with the Bible and will give us insight into what church or job or relocation we are puzzling about. These answers, however, may occasionally violate all the best of mankind's reasoning. Relationship is grown through trust, so when we trust God above circumstances, we are growing our connection with him.

There is only one major drawback to having a relationship with God. The drawback is that if he is missing, you will hurt just like Jenna did when Danielle and I left for our honeymoon. If you accept the Spirit-to-spirit connection, but then you pull back, you will feel an insatiable void. You will revisit that imprint in your spirit only to find a few old, lifeless dreams or directives, but nothing fresh or practical. You may eventually conclude that the connection you had with God never really existed, especially after circumstances run you down. Spiritual health will diminish, until physical and mental health follow closely behind—just like Jenna's tail. Your dependence may shift to rules or rituals, but without relationship, you will have no connection to God.

It is all well and good if this book can get you thinking about God—that is one of my primary objectives. But if our theorizing never moves past mental evaluation into the realm of the spiritual, we have accomplished nothing. There are certain things in life that books or instructors or psychologists cannot teach us, things that must be learned directly from God through that Spirit-to-spirit connection. Nobody has a better definition of joy or peace or happiness for your life than God. When we listen to the Holy Spirit inside us, we start to understand what God has for us specifically. When we apply this understanding through obedience, we show God that we trust him. And he, in turn, shows us the next step in obtaining the best life possible.

> But you have received the Holy Spirit, and he lives within you, so you don't need anyone to teach you what is true. For the Spirit teaches you all things, and what he teaches is true—it is not a lie. So continue in what he has taught you, and continue to live in Christ.
>
> 1 John 2:27 (NLT)

Release

Potential is a pretty hot word these days, especially in sports. As athletes go from college level to professional level, all sorts of coaches, scouts, and analysts try to determine each individual player's potential. Historically, these evaluations have been hit and miss. A few players may go on to become just as great as predicted, but most of the time, they fall disturbingly short. Disturbing, that is, to the teams that drafted them. On the other hand, sometimes the athletes dubbed "low potential" may thrive under certain conditions and actually become very valuable pick ups. There is really no exact science to determining potential. Suffice it to say that every athlete chosen for a professional sports team probably has loads of potential.

So why isn't every athlete great? Because there is a difference between *having* potential and *unlocking* potential. Many times athletes think they are something special just because they have potential—something every one of their league mates have as well. Only when this potential is unlocked and released, perhaps by the right coaching system, can an athlete and team achieve greatness. Otherwise, the athlete is just another schmo "with potential."

I have seen the same thing in my own life. When I was drinking and drugging regularly, I thought it was okay because I was still a bit sharper, more athletic, or more financially secure than some of the people around me. I thought I had so much going for me despite my addiction problems. I thought that because I had a little potential, I had something special. And although potential is nice to have, alone it gets you nowhere.

I worked part time at a liquor store for a little while during my addiction days, and I met a lot of interesting people there. Many of them had severe, life-long drinking problems that they could not escape, as evidenced by their many visits to the store per night. But the interesting part is that they all had something else that I also had—potential. I listened to many stories of musical or athletic or business careers that were "somehow" cut sadly short, typically by alcohol or drugs. I realized what a fool I was to believe that *my* potential made me special. Every Dick and Harry on the planet has potential.

Don't misunderstand me here; the specific plan God has for my life *is* special, and so is the one he has for yours. But the ability to access this plan is available to every person on earth. We all have a "best possible life we could live," and we all have a "worst possible life we could live." Most of us settle for the middle and console ourselves with the fact that we don't have the worst. But the best possible life is only accessible through God. He is the one who *unlocks* the potential…if we are willing to *release* it into his hands.

The Throw, the Chase, and the Return

Jenna is a yellow Labrador retriever. That means that retrieving runs in her blood. There is no game more fun to her than fetch, be it with a tennis ball, a Frisbee, or just your run-of-the-mill stick. The tennis ball is, of course, her favorite; she really loves to chase that thing as it bounces across the grass.

The obvious components of fetch are the throw, the chase, and the return. The first throw usually goes without a hitch, and Jenna is in hot pursuit, chasing the ball down. Once her mission is accomplished and the ball is held tightly within her jaws, she returns to me so the game can be played over and over and over until either I can't throw anymore or she can't run anymore.

It is at the tail end of "the return" that we run into a little problem. You see, Jenna loves the ball. *Really* loves it. She does not want to let go of that thing for the life of her. So she comes and stands in front of me, chomping on that ball. "Leave it," I tell her. "Release," I command. But the tennis ball represents her efforts to catch the elusive toy, and she wants to keep it.

I repeat my commands over and over, and finally she realizes, "Wait a minute, we're not playing fetch anymore." So she drops the ball, all slobbered up, and I start the fetch process over with the throw.

You would think that after a few throws, Jenna would come back and drop the ball right away. You would think that after the thousands of throws I've given her over her lifetime, she would understand how this works. But almost every time I have to tell her to "leave it" or "release," and she still takes her jolly good time. The game of fetch ceases entirely until Jenna is willing to release the ball to me.

In the last chapter, we talked about dependence on God. The major challenge of growing this dependence is that we have to decrease dependence on self, also known as independence. In order to decrease our self-dependence, there are things about ourselves we have to be willing to leave behind or release to God. In fact, we have to willingly release anything he asks, even a toy we may love dearly. If we are getting "bad vibes" in our spirit about something we own or honor, God may be asking us to release it to him, for our benefit.

God doesn't want our silly toys any more than I want Jenna's disgusting tennis ball. Willingness to release is just how "the game" is played. If we don't put anything in God's hands, what is he going to be able to work with? But if we entrust even the things we care about to him, we are going to experience the joys of life in a way that coincides with our nature at the deepest level—the spirit. We are going to realize full potential.

It takes trust—faith in my intentions—for Jenna to lay down that tennis ball for me. True, I might decide that fetch is over for the day, but I also might throw it again and again and again until Jenna herself has had enough. Either way, I am an integral part of the fetch process—it doesn't happen without me. Jenna cannot play fetch alone; I've watched her try. When Jenna is willing to accept that she is incapable of enjoying fetch on her own and to act on this realization by releasing the ball, the game of fetch can repeat itself over and over in a single day. More importantly, if she can learn to regularly give up the ball, Jenna has fetch available to her for the rest of her life—just like food and water.

Like Jenna's food and water, some things in the spirit realm can only be taken as gifts. Jenna can't earn these necessities, just like we can't earn our salvation from God. We can only accept it and let the Holy Spirit in. But as the Holy Spirit works inside of us, imprinting Godly teachings onto our often-calloused consciences, we begin to see some areas that need work. I know of a few in my life right now, and I'm sure deep down you do too. These highlighted areas are not meant to make us feel bad but rather to give us an opportunity to obey God—to make "the game" go a little smoother for us.

The more access you give a friend or family member to your life, the closer the relationship becomes. When God illuminates a deficiency in your persona, he's telling you, "I want access to that piece too." He's saying, "The box that you've given me is nice, but I want to have more reign in your life." The bottom line is that you are holding tightly onto something that is not God. The object may not necessarily be inherently evil; it's just something you're trying to grasp or fix or coddle that would go so much better if it was done God's way. Trying to do it alone is *not* the way "the game" works.

First Mate

For example, almost everyone wants the mate of their dreams. I'm not talking about pirates; I'm talking about that perfect boyfriend or girlfriend who will magically make the world a thousand times better. I know that's what I wanted—that perfect girlfriend. It was pretty easy for me to understand that I was designed for companionship, just based on my physical and mental desires. So equipped with this tiny inclination, what did I do? I forced the issue. I entered into several different relationships without even thinking about God. The results? Heartbreak and depression.

So why the miserable failure? Because getting a girlfriend was *way* more important to me than God was at that time. I hadn't even been acknowledging him. Shortly after my most difficult breakup is when I began to seek God a little more seriously. During this time, I went on dates here and there, but nothing seemed to pan out. I didn't seem to make any lasting connections. Had I lost my mojo? No, I was still ranking my desire for a girlfriend higher than I was ranking God. In other words, his opinion of a girl was second to *my* opinion of her. If God said no through my spirit but I said yes through my body or mind, then the yes won out. I handcuffed God, the one who knew exactly who I should have been with, by making all the calls myself. Again and again, my self-serving strategy always ended in defeat.

Finally, I got frustrated. I told God that he could find me a girl if he wanted and that I was sick of trying. I was actually just sick of *failing*. I started to focus on God instead of my relentless female search. And you know, suddenly the "perfect girl" crossed my path at work—my wife to be. It took a lot longer than I would have liked, mostly due to my floundering, but I finally met the woman with whom I really connected. In just over a year, we were married. Once I let go of the dilemma and let God worry about it, he took care of me very well. He unlocked my marital potential. And along the way, he taught me to trust in him a little more.

I, like most everyone else, still have so much to learn in this area. Like Jenna, I always seem to be running up to God, grasping tightly my toy of the day. But then I start to think about the drugs God pulled me out of once I resolved to let go of that lifestyle. I start to think of the wife God blessed me with once I let go of my selfish goals. I start to think about the financial blessings that have fallen in my lap once I was willing to release that cash into the offering bucket. God doesn't stop this process—I do when I start to get possessive. He's always the same—always willing to "play the game." God does not change, but he does change *you*. When I think of all the wonderful things he's already done in my life, it becomes a little easier to drop what I've been clutching so tightly.

This is how potential is unlocked—when we release whatever we have into God's hands. Certainly he has given each of us talents and abilities, and we have an American right to use those resources in whatever legal way we would like. Many people have used those talents and abilities to build careers, companies, or empires and have succeeded by unlocking varying degrees of potential. I don't discount these accomplishments at all, but truly there is only one way a talent or career or marriage can be the best it can possibly be. God must be involved to the utmost degree. In fact, to unlock ultimate potential, the whole darn thing has to be released into God's hands. That's exactly where we need to put it.

Your Story

The book of Revelation says, "And they overcame him [the evil one] by the blood of the Lamb, and by the word of their testimony; and they loved not their lives unto the death" (Revelation 12:11, KJV). God wants your potential unlocked, but we can't forget that there is an evil one who does not want living to full potential. The devil wants your story to be mundane so that you cannot have an impact on others. To overcome this mediocrity, this verse lays out three keys. The first is the blood of the Lamb—a reference to Jesus's work on the cross, which is critical to success.

The second key component is "the word of their testimony." This is your *story*. Tragedy, temptation, tempest—they're going to hit everybody. Those who give in and falter show that they have limited faith. These stories are sorrowful and tragic, stories of potential never realized. What God may have imprinted on these people's spirits was forgotten in time of trouble, and they could not overcome. But those who do get the victory are the ones who maintain specific examples that they use to overcome those trials. When difficulty strikes, the people who have ready-made, true-life, personal stories about God's goodness in their lives are going to be able to stand and overcome. As they remember and recount God's faithfulness in the past, the future doesn't look so dim, despite challenging circumstances. Their recollection of God in their lives gives them strength to overcome. As their testimony spills out, they remember again that they truly believe in God's goodness. When hard times come, they expose their faith for all to see. Their stories build their own faith, but they also inspire anyone else within earshot. A story is a powerful thing.

The final component in obtaining the victory is that "they loved not their lives to the death." In other words, they were willing to die for God's cause. This level of resolve is undoubtedly an effect of the other two components—Jesus and the strength of testimony. Now I realize we're sort of going from zero to sixty as far as religiousness when we talk about being willing to die for God. It doesn't necessarily mean you have to be willing to give your life up for God right this minute. This verse is illustrating an extreme but obtainable level of dependence on God.

As we follow God, he keeps asking for us to release more and more into his capable hands. He asks for finances and family and friendships, gently prompting us to let go of the things we hold so tightly. As we let go of more and more, the relationship gets more and more personal. Soon, God is asking for things that we don't want to let go. Of course, his intentions are entirely pure, and he is simply and continually trying to purge us of our many imperfections. As our faith grows and we begin to see this more clearly, we keep releasing our talents and abilities and resources into God's hands.

Not surprisingly, God wants more. He's never liked half-potentials or half-commitments. There is only one direction the logical progression can go. In order to make the relationship complete—as spiritually fulfilling as it can possibly be—God wants your all. He does want you to be willing to show the ultimate level of commitment—to trust him so much you would lay down your life to maintain the relationship.

If you aren't there yet, don't worry; the highly revered Apostle Peter wasn't there either when he denied he knew Jesus three times in a row. But *do* aspire. Do understand that a relationship with God is progressive, but it invariably will come down to a decision: all or nothing. You are equipping yourself to make that decision right now, but it must be made while there is breath in your human body. Are you armed with God's Spirit on the inside? Are you making realizations about God's involvement in your own personal story? You will need both in order to overcome.

> And so, dear brothers and sisters, I plead with you to give your bodies to God. Let them be a living and holy sacrifice—the kind he will accept. When you think of what he has done for you, is this too much to ask? Don't copy the behavior and customs of this world, but let God transform you into a new person by changing the way you think. Then you will know what God wants you to do, and you will know how good and pleasing and perfect his will really is.
>
> Romans 12:1-2 (NLT)

The Ritual Tricks

God speaks to us in a number of ways, be it the negative reinforcement of pain or scolding, the positive reinforcement of encouragement and blessings, or even the love in action of Jesus's sacrifice. Each communication method has its purposes, and to some degree we use them to communicate back to God. When we are mad at God, we might foolishly try to manipulate or even hurt him. When we are happy with God, we might make an effort to please him. As our understanding of him matures, we begin to base our actions less on our whimsical moods and more on what is right and wrong. Even if we can't understand all of his ways, we make sacrifices that we know he wants. We go to church even if we feel like sleeping in or going to the lake. We read our Bibles instead of watching a TV program. We give of our time to help the needy instead of going to a ball game. And oftentimes, the sacrifices we make are very pleasing to God.

Making sacrifices is an important part of a relationship with God. We must sometimes deny our feelings in order to fulfill God's purposes. But there is a level of communication that is deeper than even sacrificial action. As we talk about the Spirit-to-spirit bond that God has with us, we see that he is imprinting exactly what he wants for us on our spirit. We see that he speaks a language that can only be understood by those who are close to him. This language of love and mercy not only shows us *what* we should sacrifice, but also shows us *why*. God shows us that sacrifice is the natural reaction to having the right heart condition deep down. Sacrifice is ultimately a result of having a spirit in tune with God.

Jenna knows about four "tricks," if you can call them that. She can "sit," she can "rest" (lie down), she can "shake," and she can perform the astounding "roll over." She easily has the physical capability to accomplish these menial tasks, but she has a hard time listening to me. When I have a treat, Jenna sniffs my hand in anticipation. She needs to identify how good the treat is so that she can figure out how obedient she is going to be. Let's say this time it's a liver treat, which ranks pretty high. Jenna's first reaction is to try to pry or lick it out of my hand. For several seconds, she is entirely intoxicated by the prospect of receiving that treat.

"Jenna!" I say, usually several times, and I hold the treat up out of reach. She calms down a bit, relinquishing control to the treat-holder. When she realizes by my stance that we are entering "trick mode," she gets attentive for a minute, awaiting a command. With or without one, she springs into action.

First she sits down. No treat, so she assumes I didn't want that trick. Then she starts pawing the air to perform a one-sided hand-shake. Still no luck on the treat. To the floor she goes, first in a resting position, followed promptly by some flopping around as she tries to roll over. And yet the treat doesn't come. *What kind of cruel master is this,* she wonders, *hanging a treat out but not giving it to me? I've done everything that worked before.*

And this whole time, I haven't given one command. She has been working her butt off to try to please me with the standard trick gamut, yet she hasn't even been listening to me. She knows generally what I want, but not specifically, and she has proven very resistant to learning new tricks. This particular trick situation has played itself out in many ways in the past. I say, "Shake," and she rolls over. I say, "Roll over," and she sits. I say, "Rest," and she ignores me. And she expects to be rewarded? I would much rather she listen than work diligently to perform every trick she knows.

The same is true of our relationship with God. It is quite possible to do all sorts of actions—make a bunch of sacrifices—and yet still never truly be listening to what God specifically wants. In other words, a man can go to church all his life, give generously to the poor, be dubbed a "fine, upstanding citizen," and still be totally out of touch with God. It is very important to establish and understand what God wants generally, which is conveyed in the Bible, but if we do not move on to a point in the relationship that we begin to understand what he wants from us specifically, then our connection will be stunted. We have to be able to listen and obey.

I will never command Jenna to poop on the carpet, rip a shoe apart, or eat a pizza off the counter. These are some of the general guidelines. In the same way, God will not violate the Bible with his commands, which makes understanding the Bible very important. This is an excellent way to test the impressions you feel God has left in your spirit; they must conform to what the written Word of God says. God won't tell you to murder or steal or hate. All of his commands center on love and mercy. In fact, Jesus says the greatest two commandments are to "love God with all your heart, soul, and mind," and "love your neighbor as yourself" (Matthew 22:37, 38). He even goes on to say that "all the other commandments and all the demands of the prophets are based on these two commandments" (Matthew 22:39, NLT). Anything God truly impresses inside you will be based on this love and in harmony with the Bible. Anything else can be discarded as not from him.

The Inner Man

When Jesus walked upon this earth, he had people who were on his side, and he had people who were against him. The people on his side—his disciples—were a bunch of rag-tag fishermen and other low classers. The people who opposed him were mainly the religious icons of the day—high-class theologians, writers, and lawyers. One of the key groups that opposed Jesus to the point of ordering his crucifixion was a sect called the Pharisees. These religious types knew every facet of the books of the law, including what was prim and proper for every religious occasion and occurrence. They prayed to God, attended church, gave money, fasted, and held every custom known to the religion. Yet Jesus did not include a single one of them in his close-knit group of disciples. Why not?

Because of their *insides*. The Pharisees knew and executed the laws of God out of a matter of obligation. They were like Jenna rolling around on the floor, hoping to please me with tricks that had worked in the past. But the whole time, the Pharisees weren't listening to God at all. They were holding on to their traditions much tighter than they were to any relationship with the Father. Jesus and his disciples were much different. Jesus knew that having a spirit imprinted by God—being a man after God's own heart—was much more important than any sacrifices that could be made. He didn't teach his disciples religious customs but instead taught them how to follow God.

One day the Pharisees accused Jesus of hanging out with the riff raff. First, Jesus said, "Healthy people don't need a doctor—sick people do" (Matthew 9:12 NLT). In other words, God does not enter into relationship with people so that he can stroke our egos; he enters into relationship with us so he can help and heal us. Then Jesus added, "Now go and learn the meaning of this Scripture: 'I want you to be merciful; I don't want your sacrifices.'" (v 13). He quoted this phrase right out of their own religious book, the Old Testament.

Jesus did not mean that we should never make sacrifices as part of our walk with God. He was just saying that the condition of the heart is so much more important to God than a ritual or religious obligation. Jesus was helping the people in need not because of a religious law but because of his loving heart for them. The Pharisees were *not* helping people in need, nor showing compassion, because by their interpretation of the religious law, they didn't really have to. They weren't looking for God's specific plan for their lives; they were satisfied with generalities. Whatever God may have imprinted in their spirits was overwritten long ago with ritual memorizations. They didn't know God at all.

Jesus, on the other hand, knew exactly what God the Father wanted because of the relationship they had. This is the same kind of relationship that he taught his disciples, although some of them didn't learn much faster than Jenna does. When Jesus made the ultimate sacrifice, he didn't do it out of obligation; he did it out of love and mercy. He did it because he loved his "neighbor" as himself, and he knew we would live in eternal disparity if he didn't step in to help and heal us. So he was obedient to death—even to death on a cross (Philippians 2:8).

Laws vs. Love

Ritualism and religiousness is not something that died out with the Pharisees; it is a severe danger even today. It goes right back to the dependence issue. We as humans like to depend on something—to have something solid to grasp. By our human understanding, a system is often much easier to grasp than a relationship. A system can be static, but relationships are ever developing and ever growing. In a system, we have more control and more say. So we can have a tendency to turn a relationship with God into a religious system we depend on. The religious traditions themselves become the focal point, and we find ourselves very resistant when those traditions are challenged, even if it is God himself who is challenging them.

It would be great if we had a memo directly from God that told us how many times we had to be at church per week and how many hours of prayer and how many good deeds, and so on. That would cut out a lot of questions and add a lot of stability. But God intentionally doesn't do that. He doesn't want our dependence to shift to a memo or a ritual; he wants our dependence to remain in him. He could have made us a bunch of religious robots. But God wants a relationship, not a religious conformist. He wants you to act out of a spirit that knows his mercy, not out of obligation. He wants you to decide how much time you will give him based on your love for him, not on a recommended sacrifice amount.

It almost sounds like two different directives: first, we need to act based on what the Holy Spirit imprints, and second, we need to act based on love. But a careful comparison will reveal that these two are one and the same. Remember, everything God imprints will coincide with the love commands—loving God and loving each other. And if we are acting out of God's love, every action we perform will be exactly what God has imprinted. The Bible tells us that "love comes from God. Anyone who loves is born of God and knows God. But anyone who does not love does not know God—for God is love" (1 John 4:7-8, NLT; verses 9-21 also expand on God's love).

True love is evidence of a relationship with God. This is not a physical or mental love but a love that resides deep within the spirit—a love that has been placed by God himself. This love links us with God and causes us to desire to develop that relationship. This love links us to other believers, increasing our willingness to live unselfishly. This love links us with all mankind, prompting us to do what Jesus did to help those in desperate need, even at great personal cost. This love is what holds our world together.

God speaks to us using a great many methods, but he prefers the intimate connection of Spirit-to-spirit communication. He wants us to be close enough to him that he doesn't have to smack us with circumstances or bribe us with rewards. But no matter what method he uses, the message is always conveyed in love. He knows that if our spirits are full of his love, circumstances won't be able to pull us down. Religious systems won't be able to distract us. Our personal relationships with God will stay strong. God knows that love never fails (1 Corinthians 13:8).

I will put my laws in their minds so they will understand them, and I will write them on their hearts so they will obey them. I will be their God, and they will be my people.

Hebrews 8:10 (NLT)

Full Circle

We have seen that God is a very big-picture type of guy; he can survey the universe with a level of comprehension that we can never dream of. Yet at the same time he cares about the little things too, going so far as to express concern about each of his children's inner condition. God is doing a great work here on earth, and at the same time he is working in each of our spirits. Sometimes he does things on a grand scale, and sometimes he gives us an individual feeling of warmth or contentment that tells us he cares. He is constantly involving himself, if we can just open our eyes to see it.

One of Jenna's most endearing yet annoying habits is her "following syndrome." She basically takes turns following me and my wife everywhere we go around the apartment. If I'm collecting the trash, Jenna is on my heels. If I'm moving boxes around, Jenna is always in tow, waiting to trip me up when I turn around. Then she does a shift with my wife, following Danielle into every room as she cooks or cleans. Jenna does take a few steps back when the vacuum is turned on, but for the most part, she is always one step behind us. She has earned the nickname "the big yellow speed bump" because she is always slowing us down.

Sure, when Jenna gets in the way, it is slightly disruptive to my chore schedule. But I'll share a secret with you, as long as you don't tell Jenna: I love it! I love when she is right behind me. I love when she can't get enough of me. I love to push her aside to get through the hallway. Let's face it; I love to have Jenna involved in my life, or else I wouldn't let her be here. So when she wants to get *more* involved, even if it slows me down a little, I love it!

Jenna has a life of her own—her pleasures, her pains, and her struggles. She likes the taste of green beans. She hates when water drips on her head. She struggles with many of my commands. She is a lively dog, filled with life as she runs and jumps and plays outside. Yet she has some sort of inner desire to be a part of my life as well. She doesn't understand what I'm doing when I collect the trash or clean the apartment, but she knows she wants to be in the middle of it anyway. Her life is tied to my life.

God has a plan for my life. At the same time, God has a plan for all mankind. The way these two plans interact is of utmost importance in understanding my place in the universe. God's plan for me is unique, as is his plan for you. These plans are of great significance to the individual, which is why we have a tendency to overvalue them. If God impressed upon you to become a gardener, you may begin to believe that "gardener" is the highest calling one can have. To you it is, but in the big picture, things are a little different. In the big picture, God needs gardeners, lawyers, cab drivers, pastors, and many other workers.

God is doing something much bigger than just assigning your role. Remember the importance of love within God's plan—loving God and loving your neighbor? God is working to involve all willing participants in his big-picture plan. He wants to see as many lives thriving within a loving relationship as is possible. This is a huge, complicated work, operating at levels we cannot grasp. But there is one thing we can do. We can follow God wherever he goes.

So much focus is placed on involving God in *my* life, and perhaps that is a good way to explain the early phases of understanding. But logically we can see that my personal plan is far outranked by God's overarching plan for all of humanity. So maybe it's not so much me involving God in *my* life. Maybe it is more of me involving myself in *God's* life. When Jenna follows me around, of course there are selfish motives, but what I like is that *she* is coming to *me*. She isn't calling me to her or even expecting my responsiveness. She is looking at what I am doing, and whether she understands it or not, she is diving in. And like I said, I love it!

God will put a lot of energy into building a relationship with us; in fact, he already has. What a joy it must be for him to see us put our effort into it as well. As we talked about earlier, he wants us to be willing to lay down more and more of our lives for him. The end result of this process is the realization of the truth—that our lives aren't *ours* at all. God allows us to live in the same universe as he does. He wants us around, and he is willing to accept the inefficiencies we often bring. The least we can do is be a positive addition to his plan for humanity.

In God's story we have the privilege of choosing whether we want to be a hero or a villain. Concurrent with that decision, we choose if we will be on the winning or losing team. Many of us will fight the good fight of faith and be hand in hand with our loving Father when our final minutes come. Many more will choose to be estranged from God, be it by ignorance, rebellion, or simply by default. To those people, the commandment-toting, lightning-bolt-hurling, fun-wrecking stereotype of God will become a reality. By the rules he laid out in the Bible, God will be forced to dispel those opponents from his presence because they violated his commands yet failed to access the grace available through a relationship. To them he will seem eternally unjust and cruel, despite his best efforts to touch their hearts. Fortunately, you and I are not them, because if nothing else, we have been warned. The truth has been laid out before us; we have no excuses.

The Ten Results

Let's take a look back at those Ten Commandments of long ago—the ones we've all violated. I made an interesting realization one day as I read through them in a more contemporary translation of the Bible. I had always looked at these commandments as strict regulations on what we cannot do; "You shall not murder," "You shall not steal," "You shall not give false testimony," and so on (Exodus chapter 20, NIV). These laws are to govern the behavior of a believer, undoubtedly. But there's another way of looking at this stringent requirement system—a "back door" that gives sort of a different view.

Most people, like the Pharisees of Jesus's time, interpret the Ten Commandments as regulations; it is probably the natural way of understanding them. But what if we look at these commandments as a list of *results* instead of rules? What would these commandments be a result of? Well, a Spirit-to-spirit connection with the God who wrote them. In other words, a different way of looking at the Ten Commandments would be to say that "if you are in right relationship with God, you will not murder or steal or give false testimony." The commandments become identifiers, not rules; they identify the person who has a relationship with God.

Certainly those who have a relationship with God are not perfect at all. We need guidance just like anybody else. One aspect of the commands of the Bible is to provide that guidance. But as you look over the commands and the praises and the prophecy, there is a picture that emerges. It is not a picture of a God who slaps down regulations like they're going out of style. It is instead a picture of a human who abides perfectly by those regulations—a human who has a close-knit relationship to the Father. Most specifically, the emerging picture is that of the Son of God, Jesus, who maintained a perfect link with God the Father while roaming the planet. But generally speaking, this is the picture of the person you become as your relationship with God deepens. Jesus is our example of the way this relationship is supposed to be lived out—the way these commands become the results of a tight connection with the Father.

The Apostle Paul discusses the law at great length in the book of Romans. He says, "But now we have been released from the law, for we died with Christ, and we are no longer captive to its power. Now we can really serve God, not in the old way by obeying the letter of the law, but in the new way, by the Spirit" (Romans 7:6, NLT). So many people try to obey the law in the old way—sheer weak human willpower. But when we sacrifice self ("die with Christ"), turning ourselves over to God, the commandments are not obeyed by human will but by Godly connection within our spirits. I don't have to carry weighty regulations because my imprinted spirit does that for me. And much like a wounded spirit quickly brings those wounds to the mental and physical, so too an enlivened spirit permeates the entire being with God's life.

This doesn't mean we won't ever have to struggle with obeying the laws of God; everyone will. But if we have victory deep inside, in the spirit, we can gain that same victory on every plane. Going beyond just ourselves, we can carry that victory to higher levels within God's plan for humanity. Once we understand the power of a healthy spirit, we can truly begin to help others heal. Our true testimony will impact lives, and God's benevolence toward mankind will gain clarity. Lives will be filled with love.

God's big-picture plan is not that you save the world single-handedly, just that you do your part. There is no way to know what that part is without knowing God. There's no way to live a fulfilled life without knowing God. There is no way to reach full potential without knowing God. There is only one logical thing to do: know God.

> Thus says the Lord, "Let not a wise man boast of his wisdom, and let not the mighty man boast of his might, let not a rich man boast of his riches; but let him who boasts

boast of this, that he understands and knows me, that I am the Lord who exercises lovingkindness, justice and righteousness on earth; for I delight in these things," declares the Lord.

Jeremiah 9:23-24 (NASB)

Conclusion

I've been wrong on many occasions throughout my life. For the longest time, I thought that dogs were cute and nice and all, but they were much more trouble than they were worth. I've been funding Jenna's relaxing lifestyle for several years now; I've spent hundreds of dollars on this dog, if not thousands. And let me tell you, I was so wrong! Having Jenna around has been worth every penny. Given a choice, I might have said no to having a dog. Good thing my wife didn't give me a choice.

I have learned so much about relationships from Jenna, my silly dog. Relationships can be so complex, but Jenna kicks those complexities to the curb. Our relationship is simple: one person plus one dog. That dog loves this person so much that every greeting is enthusiastic. Every affectionate gesture is appreciated. Every possible minute of attention is craved. And I love that dog so much that every need is met, even the ones she can't understand. Treats rain upon that dog. That dog's future is secure. My life is richer because of Jenna, and Jenna's life is fuller because of me.

But there's another thing I was totally wrong about: God. I never would have guessed that he would want to have a relationship with a human—and more specifically, *this* short-falling human. But he does. I know this not only because I have reasoned my way through some of it but because I am in that relationship right now. I don't bring much to the table—perhaps some enthusiastic pursuit and appreciation—but God still wants me around. And he meets my needs. He blesses me. He gives me a place in his life for all eternity.

I have described my progression in the understanding of God, but the story is only partially written. God is still working on my story, and he's still working on yours. My understanding doesn't stop when I type the last period of this book, and yours doesn't stop when you reach that period. It can't—that's not how a relationship works. A relationship must be continually built and strengthened, or else it turns into a ritual or obligation. Dissolution isn't far beyond that.

So keep on chasing after God! You will not be disappointed. Just as the dog was designed to be a companion to man—"man's best friend"—so too was man designed to be a companion to God. We cannot be complete without him. Embrace your role. You were designed to be "God's best friend!"

Salvation Prayer

If you want to get right with God by accepting Jesus into your heart, pray this prayer in sincerity:

> Heavenly Father, I believe in my heart that Jesus is your Son, and I believe Jesus died for my sins. God, I repent for all my sins and ask that you forgive me. I believe that you raised Jesus from the dead, and I confess with my mouth Jesus as my Lord and Savior. Now I am saved. I have chosen life, and I am heaven bound. In the name of Jesus, Amen.
>
> —Salvation prayer written by Reverend Matthew T. Mangan.

About the Author

Clay Cornelius lives in Lansing, Michigan with his wife, Danielle, and their loveable yellow Lab, Jenna. They are members of Mount Hope Church. Clay has graduated from the Mount Hope Church Bible Training Institute and is currently teaching classes there. In his spare time, he enjoys playing basketball and working out. His motivation for writing is to help his Christian brothers and sisters advance in their understanding of all that God has for them. He has previously published *The Committee*, a creative biographical account of the deliverance leading up to his acceptance of Jesus Christ.

The Cornelius household has changed since the completion of this book. They have moved from their apartment into a new house, which Jenna kindly christened on her first visit by pooing in the basement (some things never change). They have welcomed Rhubarb, the energetic chocolate Lab puppy, into their home. And finally, Danielle has given birth to the Cornelius's first child, Abigail Ruth. Clay and Danielle credit all of these wonderful blessings to their loving Father and Savior.

Clay would love to hear from you. If you enjoyed his book, hated it, or would like more information or pictures of Jenna, please e-mail Clay directly at:

claypcornelius@gmail.com

or write him at:
Clay Cornelius
P.O. Box 80106
Lansing, MI 48908

He would love to hear your comments, questions, or criticisms. Please write!